MAIL ORDER MOMENTS

CISSIE M. PATTERSON

Margaret,

I hope you enjoy Simon and Ida Mae's story! Cissie Patterson

INTRODUCTION

Struggling to define her future, Ida Mae Miller enlists the help of her sister, Elizabeth, to escape a violent relationship. Could becoming a mail order bride be her answer for a new life? One letter touches her heart. Seattle is far enough away —she hopes. Simon Farmer has spent three years reliving what happened in his past. Could he have done anything to change what occurred? His mother, Harriett, convinces him a mail order bride is what he needs to move on. Will his plea inspire the right woman to marry him? Set in Kirsten Osbourne's world of Beckham, Harriett, Simon's mother, and Elizabeth, Ida's sister, reunite as they help a survivor and a heartbroken lawyer find a future together, while the past tries to drive them apart.

ACKNOWLEDGMENTS

A huge thank you to Bobbie Sue Brown, Erin Krol, Tracy Lewis, Amy Petrowich, and Lorena Rodgers for taking the time to beta read my first book and offering feedback and encouragement for a better story.

A special thank you to Sara Jolene, an amazing author and friend who took the time to provide her input toward a much better story.

To Kirsten Osbourne – thank you for pushing me to write this story and allowing me to play with the characters in your world. Your support and guidance is much appreciated. Words cannot express how much.

To the authors in the Pioneer Hearts Facebook group – thank you for your historical western romance stories and encouraging me to write. You put up with my crazy ideas, tolerate my input and make me smile with every story you write. All of you inspire me with your amazing talents and beautiful stories.

To the Peppermint Penguins – you know how you are and thanks for
listening to me. You keep my crazy in check.

CHAPTER 1

BECKHAM, MASSACHUSETTS – APRIL 1909

*I*da Mae Miller knocked on her sister's door at 300 Rock Creek Road, as she wiped the tears from her face. She knew it was late and she probably looked a mess but she had nowhere else to go. If Elizabeth wouldn't take her in, Stefan would find her quickly. Even God couldn't help her then. She peeked in the side window and knocked again. She would keep on knocking until someone answered the door.

It took several minutes and several more knocks before Elizabeth opened the door, wearing her dressing gown and looking disheveled. "What in the world? Ida Mae, what's wrong?"

"May I come in?" Ida Mae said urgently, looking around. "Please. I have nowhere else to go."

"Of course!" Elizabeth ushered her in and shut the door. "You're always welcome. Come in and we can talk."

Ida quietly followed her to the large office used for

matchmaking services. They sat on the sofa and Elizabeth pulled her into her embrace.

Ida couldn't hold back any longer as she let loose a stream of tears. They sat that way for several minutes while Elizabeth held her and rubbed her back.

"It's all right, let it out. We can talk when you're ready. I'm always here for you. You're safe here."

Elizabeth saw the door to her office open and her husband, Bernard, quietly walked inside with two cups of hot tea and milk. He winked at her as he quietly set the tray down on the table next to the sofa. He tiptoed back out of the room.

Ida Mae wiped at her eyes with the back of her hand as Elizabeth gave her a handkerchief. She blew her nose and sighed.

"You deserve to know everything. You've always been the sister I could turn to whenever I needed to talk."

"My door is always open. Over the years, I've watched you mature and grow into a lovely young woman. There were times, many times in fact, that I wasn't sure what would become of my demon horde siblings but you've made me proud. I'll be sorry when Stefan marries you and takes you away to Boston."

Ida's eyes filled with tears again. She knew this wouldn't be easy, but as she was inviting danger into Elizabeth's home, she had to tell her sister. Ida didn't think she would want to stay if it meant any harm would come to Elizabeth's family.

"Stefan and I won't be getting married. I've run away, and I dread him ever finding me. I don't know what he would do."

Elizabeth looked at her in confusion. "What's going on? Did Stefan do something?"

Ida took off her coat and rolled up her left sleeve. Ugly,

purple bruises covered her wrist and her lower arm. Elizabeth gasped.

"He's a brute, a most evil creature. It started off innocently, with him making comments about who I went to tea with, or who I looked at in church. He accuses me of vile things and calls me hateful names. He leaves bruises on me in places that cannot be seen. I haven't told anyone because Stefan says that he will harm those I love most."

Ida sobbed but caught herself. She took a deep breath and continued, "About four months ago, he began striking out at me whenever he felt I was less than a perfect fiancée. He has hit me on several occasions but the past two days, he has followed me to the diner and has been waiting for me when I got off work. That's why I snuck out of my room at the boarding house tonight. I can't escape him, and I must get away. I need you to help me, dear sister. I need you to hide me!"

Elizabeth angrily looked at Ida. "Absolutely! His behavior is inexcusable. Stefan was so nice and polite to our family and to you in public. You can hide here until you're ready to decide what you want to do next in your life. I'll speak to Bernard and we'll keep you safe. Benjamin and Eleanora will be thrilled to spend some time with their favorite aunt."

An hour later, Ida settled into a small bedroom on the third floor. She left her things in a bag on the floor to wait until morning and crawled into bed. She was safe and her secret was out. Nothing else mattered at the moment.

~

SEATTLE, *Washington – April 1909*

Simon leaned back in his chair and closed his eyes. Three years had passed since that fateful day. He'd only been twenty years old, fresh out of law school, when he joined the

Law Offices of Stewart, Stevens, and Gorvin. He was lucky to have gotten such an important start to his law career, but courting the daughter of Mr. Gorvin might have played a role in his luck. He had met her at the university. Debra had been full of life and laughter. Theirs was to be a grand wedding – the event to remember in all of San Francisco for years to come. Life, however, is an ever twisting path and along the way, Debra's path took another turn. Simon shook his head. He wasn't going to spend more time dwelling on something he couldn't change.

A knock at his front door startled him from his memories. He stood up and walked out of the parlor to open the door.

"Why, hello, Mother, to what do I owe this surprise?"

Simon's mother took off her hat and stepped inside to give her son a hug. "It's been so long since I've seen you that I wanted to stop by and make sure everything was all right."

Simon and his mother sat on the couch in the front parlor. "Can I offer you anything to drink? Mrs. Picklebottom is off today, but she made some wonderful lemonade yesterday."

"No, dear. I wanted to ask if you'd like to come to dinner tonight with your father and me at the house? We'd like to sit down together and discuss a proposition with you."

"You aren't planning on having any young ladies at this dinner again, are you? I'm not interested in courting anyone."

"Sweetheart, it's been three years. Debra's not coming back. I think it's time for you to consider opening your heart to someone else. I know it isn't easy for you. But you deserve a bit of happiness in your life. The right woman is out there for you. But to answer your question - no, there won't be any young ladies at our table this evening. Tonight is for you. We miss you, son."

After promising to show up, Simon kissed his mother

good-bye and decided to rest a bit before dinnertime. Reminiscing about the past always seemed to drain him of his energy. Would he ever move beyond remembering? Maybe his mother was right. Maybe moving on and finding a special lady would help him forget what had happened. ·

Three hours later, Simon sat at the dinner table with his mother and father. His youngest brother and two of his sisters were at his Aunt Mary's house. They loved to visit with cousin Rose's children and Aunt Mary didn't seem to mind a houseful of chaos, having had eight children of her own and numerous grandchildren.

"How is Annabelle doing? She must be excited to be a mother soon." Simon asked his mother about his eldest sister. He wasn't particularly interested in the answer but wanted to push off the topic his mother would bring up as long as possible.

"Yes, only four more months and we'll finally be grandparents." Harriett reminisced. "I remember when you were born. Time flies by so quickly. And your sister Florence is enjoying her time as governess of the Crider children in Beaver Creek. My three eldest have grown up and flown the nest, but now you're back in Seattle and we're concerned. It's been three years."

"I wish you'd come help me with the lumber mill. It's been too long since you've visited, son." Max Farmer took his wife's hand. "Your mother and I are worried about you."

Simon was annoyed. "I think I have the right to work through all that happened in my own time. I am not ready to get married and settle down. I'm not ready to jump back into life with a smile, pretending that nothing happened. I'm managing this the best I can." Simon ran a hand through his hair in frustration.

Harriett jumped in. "I know you don't think you're ready to court someone. The pain is still there. What happened was awful, and it hurt you deeply." Harriett took a deep breath. "You know that over twenty years ago, I ran a mail-order bride business in Beckham, Massachusetts. My successor, Elizabeth Tandy, still runs that business and manages the *Grooms' Gazette*."

Harriett looked at Simon lovingly. "She's done an amazing job matching up couples that, at one time, felt as downhearted as you. Would you consider writing her a letter and allowing her to help you find a bride? I believe a life partner would be the healing you need to move forward with your life."

"Do you really think that would be fair? She would be expecting love and happiness. I can't promise those things." Simon paused to think. "Although, I do admit, it would be nice to have someone to talk to besides myself. I wouldn't mind giving up some of the household chores to someone else either." He took a sip of water to calm himself. "It doesn't seem fair to offer companionship without love though."

"Marriages have been built on much less. Many of the women I helped were escaping bad situations. They were aware that love is not a guarantee, but rather a hope for something that may happen. You wouldn't be disappointing a young lady if you're honest and upfront about what you're looking for and what your expectations are. Every woman appreciates honesty in a relationship."

Simon looked at his parents holding hands and smiling at each other. He wanted that. He wanted a woman who would gaze up at him with love shining in her eyes. A woman who would hold his hand as they sat on the porch under the stars. A woman he could support and laugh with as their children ran around them. He thought he'd had that with Debra but other forces were stronger than love.

"I'll consider it. I know you want what's best for me. I can't promise more than that."

Harriett nodded. "That's all we can ask. I came from an impossible situation in my first marriage. I never thought love was something I would find. Fate has a way of turning the impossible into the possible. Never give up on your dreams and God will find a way to make everything better."

Simon went home after dinner and thought long into the night about what his mother had said. She had shared her story with her children from a young age. As Harriett Long, she'd survived an abusive marriage that ended in the loss of her unborn child and resulted in her crippled leg. She'd found the courage to survive and Simon was proud of the woman she had become. She enjoyed volunteering her time managing the battered women's shelter and had helped countless women.

The next morning, after a long and restless night, Simon knew what he would do. He would honor his mother and stop dwelling on the past. He had to begin moving forward. At the very least, he would enjoy the companionship of someone else. He sat down at his desk and wrote a letter to Mrs. Elizabeth Tandy.

CHAPTER 2

*I*da Mae tidied up the kitchen as she finished preparations for lunch. It was Cook's day off and Ida enjoyed helping Elizabeth around the house. Benjamin and Eleanora had enjoyed an early lunch and gone off with their father to pick up supplies at the general store. Nora always enjoyed the stick of penny candy that Bernard secretly bought her when he thought Elizabeth wasn't looking. Elizabeth and Bernard had a solid, loving relationship. Ida smiled and thought to herself - *Why couldn't Stefan have been more like Bernard?*

A month passed and Stefan had shown up at the house several times, demanding the return of Ida Mae like she was his possession. Stefan would knock on the door and scream loudly enough for everyone in the house to hear, "You can't get away from me, I won't let you." Each time, Bernard answered the door and firmly told him that they hadn't seen her in weeks.

Ida remained hidden and didn't leave the house. She was getting quite tired of being cooped up inside, but it was the safest plan. She was even afraid to go out into the back garden, in case Stefan was spying through the fence. Ida hoped that coming from a family of fourteen Miller children, Stefan would spend his time confused as to which home she had run to. Eventually, he would give up and move on with his life. He had to — she wasn't going back to an abusive relationship.

As she went into the hallway on her way to let Elizabeth know lunch was almost ready, Ida picked up the mail from the small table by the front door. Elizabeth liked to go through each letter for the *Grooms' Gazette* with her and get her opinion on the various grooms. She suspected Elizabeth was up to more than that but she did enjoy spending time with her sister. She also found the letters interesting and began daydreaming about what a life out West would be like – a life away from Stefan's control. She knocked on the office door and stepped in to deliver the mail.

"Look, two new letters arrived today. That makes eight this week alone! I had no idea this mail-order bride business of yours was so popular."

Elizabeth looked up from her desk and smiled. "There are lots of good men in this world. My job is to find each one the woman who suits him. Give your heart another chance, and when the time is right, he'll be there waiting for you. There's something I've been wanting to show you."

Ida looked at her sister as her eyes teared up. While her bruises had all but healed, her heart had not. She wasn't sure if, or when, she would be ready to love again. In the meantime, she had to figure out how to continue on with her life while avoiding Stefan.

Elizabeth got up from her chair and went over to the closet. She pulled out a box filled with letters. "This is something that I've been saving for a long time. I want to read you one special letter. It was addressed to Harriett Long, my predecessor. Several years ago, she traveled west to be a mail-order bride herself. She returned the matchmaker letters she had received from past brides and asked me to keep them as part of the mail order moments we have shared together."

Elizabeth sat on the couch with Ida, as she opened the box. Inside was a pile of envelopes that she had collected over the years. She took out the envelope on top and pulled out a letter. She began to read it aloud to Ida.

1888 – Hudspeth, Iowa

Dear Harriett,

It's been five years since I accepted your mail-order bride proposal and traveled to Iowa to marry John Powers. So much has changed in my life during that time that I wanted to write and update you. You know, it was difficult going against my parents and fleeing their control. Horace Templeton was an evil man and I'm glad I escaped marrying him. I don't regret his being shot dead by the sheriff. I'm still not sorry, and I won't ever pretend to be.

Life with him as my husband would have been empty, and I would have been controlled in all I did. John has shown me the love and patience that I needed to truly escape that control. The mind holds us within a cell that we sometimes feel we cannot escape. I hope as my children grow that I do not force them into anything that makes them feel trapped. Each one of us deserves love and promise and laughter within the walls of a home.

Our family is growing and my heart is filled with joy. John and I have two boys, Georgie and Jeremiah, and a newborn daughter, Kristina. I couldn't have imagined this for myself five years ago. I am so happy to have found this man who completes me. Thank you so much for helping me escape my situation and learn how to live again. I would recommend your services to any woman who needs to start over or begin anew. The mail-order bride route was exactly what I needed, even if I didn't know it at the time. Good men do exist out there and we must search for that which we deserve. I will never forget you, my friend, for assisting in my time of need. May God bless you and your family.

Your grateful friend,

Maude (Abernathy) Powers

Ida wiped a tear from her eye and smiled at Elizabeth. "Thank you for sharing. I know I cannot allow my past to control my future. I have left Stefan but I haven't really escaped him, have I? He is still ruling my thoughts and deeds. Perhaps I need to leave Beckham and get as far away from him as possible."

Elizabeth took Ida's hand and patted it gently. "I believe you need to leave Beckham to find freedom. I'd never place you in a situation where you'd be in danger. I know it feels hopeless, but you're not alone."

"I know. Thank you for being there for me." Ida said, as she stood and placed the mail on the desk. "Lunch will be ready in ten minutes. I'll let you read your letters while I finish preparing the lunch."

Elizabeth nodded as she glanced at the letters. "Oh! This one is from Harriett Farmer. Harriett is the original match-maker, the one I told you about, who gave me my start. We still correspond occasionally. I'll catch up with her and be there shortly for lunch."

Ten minutes later, Elizabeth joined Ida in the dining room. As Ida poured the lemonade, Elizabeth smiled at her. "Shall I say grace?" Ida sat and held Elizabeth's right hand in hers. She bowed her head and closed her eyes.

"Dear Lord, thank you for the meal we are about to receive. Thank you for bringing my sister into this home and guiding her onto the path you set before her. Help her heart to heal, Lord, and open her mind to all you place before her. Bless my family and keep them safe. Amen."

After their lunch of cucumber sandwiches, boiled eggs, and rice-pudding, Elizabeth glanced at Ida and placed two letters on the table. Ida looked at her curiously. "As I told you, I received a letter from Harriett Farmer, my predecessor. It was an interesting update. I'd like you to read it and let me know your thoughts, if you don't mind."

Ida took the letter from Elizabeth's outstretched hand and began to read,

1909 – Seattle

My dearest Elizabeth,

It has been some time since I've written to you. I hope you are not running out of brides in Beckham, although I suspect you are not. Women still look for love and the west is a strong provider of men. I write this letter to update you on the latest in Seattle.

Max and I are extremely proud of our six children. Our daughter, Annabelle, will finally make us grandparents by the end of the summer and we are truly excited! Florence has begun a governess job for a family in Beaver Creek, about an hour's drive from here. She loves the little ones and hopes to find a husband one of these days. My three youngest are busy in school and are quite the handful! But, it is my son, Simon, which drives me to write this letter to you.

Simon is now twenty-three years old. He lived in San Francisco three years ago and was engaged to a lovely young lady. Unfortunately, fate had a different path for him and he is back living in Seattle. These three years have been hard for him. Simon and I have spoken and I have urged him to contact you. He is considering a mail-order bride as his future. Given what occurred, he isn't looking for love at this moment. You and I, however, know that God often places His hand on these matches and guides our steps. Please help Simon find the wife he needs. I am confident Beckham holds what his heart desires.

Once he finds the courage to write the letter, I'd like him not to wait. I am enclosing the funds for your services, a ticket to Seattle and some spending money for her trip. Please send his bride as soon as Simon finds the courage to ask and a match is found.

Your partner in Seattle,

Harriett

Ida took a deep breath and sighed. "She obviously loves her son and is concerned for his welfare," Ida said softly. "What is it you need from me?"

Elizabeth looked at her and handed Ida the second letter. "This is the other letter I received today. It is from Simon Farmer, looking for a wife. I'd like you to read it. I think your opinion would be important in helping him find a partner."

To my future helpmate,

Are you feeling like all is hopeless? You are not alone. The past is filled with nightmares of memories we cannot change. I have spent three years trying to outrun my sorrows. I am not ready to love but I am ready to live. If you understand that, you are the bride for me.

If you are able to cook and keep house, are between the ages of eighteen and twenty-three, and wish to escape your situation (no questions asked) then I would like to correspond with you. I live in the Seattle area, in the state of Washington.

I am twenty-three years old, educated at a university in California, and willing to work alongside you to build a future. A wish for laughter and friendship is preferable. A desire to have children is a bonus. If this interests you, please reply to me.

Simon Farmer

Ida wiped a tear away from the corner of her eye. She stood up and walked over to look out the window. She sighed and stared out at the blue sky, imagining that she had the freedom to walk out into the sunshine as she used to. She closed her eyes and recalled the fear as Stefan berated her for allowing the sun to beat down on her skin, coloring it a tinge too red. Ida took a deep breath. "I'll do it. I'll go."

Elizabeth stood and walked over to her sister. She reached over and took Ida's hand, squeezing it, as she gazed out the window with her. "And I'll go with you. I have been wanting an adventure. Benjamin and Nora can stay with Bernard as he runs the business in my absence. I'd love to see Harriett again and I can't deliver my sister to a man without meeting him myself. This way, Bernard can distract Stefan and he won't realize that you have left or look for you outside of Beckham."

Ida bit her lip, pausing for a moment to gather her emotions. "Then let me write a letter to Simon and start preparing for the journey. How long do you think we need before we go?"

Elizabeth smiled. "A week should be enough. Now, let's figure out how I'm going to convince Bernard to let me go on this adventure with you."

～

Two weeks later...

Ida Mae looked out the window as the train entered the last leg of its journey. The Northern Pacific Railway, with its Pullman-Standard cars, offered some of the finest dining that could be found via rail. The cars were lit with electricity and equipped with every comfort imaginable. It had been an education to travel through this country so rich in history and stare in awe at the beauty of God's creation around them.

Bernard had insisted that she and Elizabeth take the new train service offered to the public from Chicago, by way of St. Paul and Minneapolis, to the Great Northwest. An observation car was attached to the train and further enhanced the breathtaking views. Elizabeth noted that the modern Pullman sleeping car made train travel much more bearable than it had been for their oldest sister, Susan. Ida was surprised it only took two days to make it from Beckham to Chicago by rail. Rumor had it that a faster route was to begin shortly that could make the trip in only twenty-five hours.

Their journey to Seattle from Chicago was a three-day schedule; however, Elizabeth and Ida Mae opted to stay over in Yellowstone Park. They spent two days touring the park. It was the trip of a lifetime for both, and Ida knew she would never forget the view of Old Faithful Geyser shooting boiling water over 100 feet into the air. She had seen wildlife that had only existed for her previously in books.

Tomorrow, they would arrive in Seattle. Ida hoped that Simon would be waiting for them, however, they did not wait for his reply to her letter before they'd left. Elizabeth sent a letter to Harriett Farmer before they departed Beckham. Bernard had been difficult to convince but he finally agreed to the plan, provided they take the newer train route that was quickly building a reputation for safety.

Elizabeth looked at her and smiled. "Are you nervous? Tomorrow is a big day."

Ida nodded and looked out the window. "I am scared. I think I'd rather face a hungry bear or one of those wild bison in Yellowstone than step off this train."

Elizabeth laughed and hugged her sister. "You know, Susan was scared when she became a mail-order bride. At the same time, it was madness at home with eleven children. I know you weren't born yet, but that's where the demon horde got their name. Susan traveled to meet Jesse Dailey but when she got there, she found out he had been killed. It was a scary time for her. In fact, I have a letter she wrote with me. I thought it might be helpful to you." Elizabeth reached into her bag and took out the letter.

1885

Dearest sister Elizabeth,

Oh my stars, what a crazy trip this has been! When I arrived in Fort Worth, I found that my intended, Jesse Dailey, had been killed.

His brother, David, offered to take me as his bride. Unknown to me, David has four children – all boys – and just as awful as the demon horde I left behind! I could not believe that I had hoped for no children and instead I got four rascals.

A year has gone by and I wouldn't trade my life for anything. What I had hoped and dreamed for is completely different than what I received, but at the same time, it's not. I dreamed of quiet nights under the stars, love that every woman desires, and a lifetime of happiness. God has blessed me with all of that and much more! My days are full of life and laughter, my heart is full of blessings, and our family is rich in love. I may not have gotten what my heart desired in 1884 but God has granted my every wish. Please thank Harriett Long for her role in connecting me with David Dailey in Fort Worth and I hope that you find your happiness in life as well.

With much affection,

Susan (Miller) Dailey

P.S. I am pregnant and if she is a girl, I hope to name her Harriett after all she has done for me.

Ida smiled. "I am so glad things worked out for Susan. With her being the oldest and me being the youngest, I don't have the connection with her that you do. I never knew that's who she named our niece after. And to think, she had three more children after that."

Elizabeth nodded. "The path before us sometimes seems dark but I promise, there is light along the way. I will make sure Simon Farmer is exactly what you need before I leave you with him. It's my duty as your sister. I need to see you smile again."

CHAPTER 3

Simon Farmer stood with his mother, Harriett, at the train station. Today was the day his mail-order bride arrived, accompanied by her sister, matchmaker Elizabeth Tandy. He had been surprised that the matchmaker was accompanying his bride, but his mother had been absolutely ecstatic to connect with her old friend. He was quite nervous about meeting his bride. Her letter had been hurried but yet spoke volumes. He took it out and read it again.

Simon,

I am twenty-two years old and I recall laughter in my life. Perhaps I shall find it again in Seattle. I am able to cook quite well and am agreeable to children if so blessed.

Unfortunately, my nightmares are not memories and alone is the only safe place to be at the moment. We cannot outrun sorrow. Rather, we must learn to move beyond that which we cannot change. Perhaps we can learn how to face the future together.

My sister will be accompanying me on the train as she wishes to visit an old friend in the Seattle area. We leave in a week and will travel from Chicago via the Northern Pacific Railway. Expenses have been covered already. By the time you read this, we will be on

the way and shall arrive on the fifth of June. I look forward to
being your friend as we forge on into our tomorrows.

   Kind regards,

   Ida Mae Miller

   Simon looked up as the train came into view and placed the folded letter into his suit coat. He removed his hat and clutched it in front of him. He was nervous to meet a strange woman. He hoped she didn't expect a kiss in greeting. The memory of Debra danced across his mind, and he closed his eyes. What was he doing? What made him think that he was ready to accept another woman into his life?

   "Breathe, Simon, breathe." Harriett said as she touched his arm. "One step at a time. You haven't met her yet, and from what you told me from her letter, she has demons of her own to battle. You'll be able to grow together and form a relationship based on the future and not the past."

   Simon opened his mouth to answer when he saw a strikingly attractive older woman getting off the train, followed by a beautiful blonde with the face of an angel. She was wearing a light blue dress with a white shawl around her shoulders. He was momentarily stunned by how lovely she was. Her eyes darted left and right as if she was expecting someone to jump out at her. He swallowed hard and wondered if he had gotten in over his head. He hadn't expected to see such an exquisite woman answer his ad. He'd expected an unattractive spinster, making it easier for him to maintain his distance.

   Elizabeth got off the train first, with Ida Mae standing behind her. She scanned the crowd for her old friend, Harriett Farmer. It had been twenty-four years, but she was confident she would recognize her.

   "Elizabeth! Yoo-hoo, Elizabeth!" A fifty-year old woman, with graying hair and a pronounced limp, waved and began working her way through the crowds of people on the platform. Simon walked behind his mother, wondering what he should say to this stunning female.

Elizabeth smiled and waved back. She took Ida's hand and said, "Come on, let's meet your future mother-in-law and groom." They began maneuvering through the crowds toward Harriett.

"My goodness, it sure is crowded in Seattle. Do you think there's always this many people at the train station?" Ida said, surprised at how little room there was to move. She had pictured a bustling town, but so far, Seattle appeared even busier than Boston.

As Elizabeth and Harriett embraced each other in a joyous hug, Ida saw the most ruggedly handsome man she had ever seen, with dark hair and a strong jawline. He stood there awkwardly, holding his hat in his hand, staring at her with his mouth slightly open. He finally spoke and held out his hand. "Simon Farmer at your service, Miss. Are you Ida Mae Miller?"

Ida nodded and shook his hand. "Hello, Simon. It's very nice to meet you. I've heard so much about your mother from Elizabeth that I feel I already know her." She smiled at him, tentatively, her throat going dry. What if he wasn't as nice as he looked? What if evil lurked behind those deep blue eyes? What if he was the same as Stefan? God help her, what would she do?

Simon winked at her and Ida pulled back slightly. She went still, like a deer who smells a hunter in the wind. "Miss Miller?" Simon said. "Are you okay?"

Elizabeth stepped forward, putting her arm around Ida, and held out her hand. "You must be Simon. You've grown from the little boy I used to hear about in your mother's letters. I'm Elizabeth Tandy —Ida's sister and your matchmaker."

"Good afternoon, Mrs. Tandy." Simon said, with a twinkle

in his eye. "My mother has spoken very highly of you and the work that you have done matching couples."

"Please, call me Elizabeth. After all, we'll be family soon."

Harriett took a step forward and wrapped Ida in a warm hug. "You must be Ida, the youngest Miller child. Do they still call your siblings the demon horde?"

Ida nodded and laughed, feeling entirely at ease with this woman who was to be her future mother-in-law. "Yes, ma'am. I'm afraid their antics have become legendary in Beckham and it is difficult to escape the name. I fear the stories have become larger than life and are quite exaggerated now."

Harriett took Ida's hand and said, "Well, welcome to Seattle. I look forward to getting to know you better." Harriett took Elizabeth's hand in her other hand. "I'm so glad that you have come to visit, Elizabeth. We have much to catch up on."

Simon chimed in, "I'll just grab your bags and we can be on our way, ladies. June first was the start of Exposition, the World's Fair right here in Seattle, and it's been extraordinarily busy this week. The fair is publicizing the development of the Pacific Northwest. We figured we'd take you back to her home to settle in and wash up. We'll have time to become better acquainted after you've had a chance to rest a bit."

Simon looked at Ida, and as their eyes met, he smiled again. Her beautiful blue eyes were filled with curiosity and something that resembled fear. As she looked away, Simon frowned. He was surprised at his desire to protect her and he hoped he could help her lose that wariness in her eyes. He was certain that whatever she was hiding, they would fight their past demons together.

～

IDA BREATHED DEEPLY as she looked around Seattle. Elizabeth and Harriett chattered like a pair of crows behind her in the carriage, as they caught up on days gone by. It was comforting that at least her mother-in-law was known to Elizabeth and was a safe haven for Ida. On the train, Elizabeth had told her about Harriett's role in the battered women's shelter in Seattle and assured her that Harriett would be her champion. No harm would come to her with Harriett around.

As she gazed around at the bustling city, Simon pointed out various items of interest. "It's beautiful. I had no idea that Seattle was such a large city." Ida marveled. "It's not at all what I imagined the west would look like." She looked everywhere around her, her eyes lit with excitement.

Simon laughed. "Seattle is not much different than the East. The buildings are new, but there's over two hundred thousand people in the city. In fact, President Taft recently stayed at the newly opened Sorrento Hotel. We even have cars competing for space on the streets now."

Ida looked at him with wide eyes. "My brother-in-law, Bernard, drives a car but I haven't ridden it. Do you have one?"

"No, not yet. My father has one and I have driven his." Simon said. "Did you know they can travel four miles an hour? Perhaps one day I can take you for a drive."

"Oh, that would be exciting. I'm learning to live one day at a time because the future can change in the blink of an eye." Ida said. She gave Simon a tentative smile as the carriage hit a bump in the road. Simon reached over and grabbed Ida's hand to steady her.

"Oh my goodness," Ida laughed nervously. "I wasn't expecting that bump. Thank you for steadying me." Her heart was racing wildly from his touch. "Tell me about yourself. Why did you send for a wife?"

Simon was at a loss for words. The moment his hand touched hers, an electric spark travelled up his arm. Her touch was as light as a feather, yet as powerful as an earthquake to the depths of his soul. The comforting touch of a woman was something he had not experienced in three years. Not since Debra... Simon shook his head. No, he wouldn't think about that right now. The past couldn't be changed. He let go of her hand and focused on the horses and the road in front of them.

"I have no one to come home to and my house feels empty. After a short stay in San Francisco, I moved back to Seattle and three years later, it still doesn't feel like home." Simon took a deep breath. "I found myself wishing that I had someone to share my life with, someone I could laugh with and share warm meals with after a long day of work."

"What type of work do you do?" Ida asked. She tried to focus on the drive, but she kept glancing over at him. She could still feel where their hands had touched. She wanted to take his hand in hers, but she didn't want to appear too forward. There was something trustworthy about this man, but she had made a mistake before. His gentle character could be hiding a monster beneath the surface, waiting for an angry word to rouse the beast within.

"I am a lawyer with the city of Seattle. It is an interesting line of work and I enjoy watching the population grow and assisting in making the laws that govern the great people of this city." Simon stated with such pride that Elizabeth jumped into the conversation.

"How exciting! You didn't mention that your son had grown into such an important man."

Harriett laughed. "Oh, I don't know about important. More often than not, I have to remind him how special he is. He's the most humble soul I've ever met. He needs a caring wife to show him how special he is. I'm glad such a lovely woman answered his letter."

Simon blushed but was saved from answering as they arrived at Harriett's home. He stopped the carriage in front of a large white house. His father, Max, came out to welcome them and help carry in their bags. Simon was proud of his father and hoped one day he would be half the husband his father was. His father helped his mother down from the carriage, automatically protecting her crippled leg. He then gave his hand to help Elizabeth down as he said, "It's nice to meet both of you. Harriett has been talking non-stop about your visit to Seattle."

Simon came around the carriage and held out a hand to Ida to assist her down. As she took his hand and took a step, her foot slipped and she tumbled forward slightly. Simon moved his hands to her waist and caught her and gently lowered her to the ground. Her lips were inches away and her wide eyes gazed into his. "Oh, I'm so sorry," she murmured.

"I'm not," he said and winked at her.

Ida playfully tapped his chest with her hand. "Oh, stop that." Her cheeks burned pink with embarrassment.

Harriett and Elizabeth exchanged a smile and headed inside the house. Simon held Ida's elbow and led her inside. Harriett led them to a small parlor down a hallway. "Please come in and sit down." Harriett said, indicating a small couch and two parlor chairs. Elizabeth sat in one chair, as Harriett sat in the other. Simon led Ida over to the open couch, and the two of them sat down.

"I'm sure you'd both like to rest after your journey," Harriett said. "Would you care for a light lunch first? I believe Cynthia, our maid, has put together some sandwiches for us."

"That would be lovely, thank you." Ida said. "Could we freshen up quickly before lunch?"

"Absolutely. Simon, would you show Ida to her room? It's the first room on the left at the top of the stairs. Elizabeth will be using the room at the end of the hall on the right."

Simon motioned toward the stairs. "Follow me, ladies. I'll show you to your accommodations."

Elizabeth rubbed a handkerchief across her forehead. "I think I'll stay behind and help Harriett. I'll be up shortly."

Ida followed Simon up the stairs. "This way," Simon said. "I hope you like it." At the top of the stairs, he opened the door on the left.

A beautiful hand-carved bed was against the wall and a light-blue quilt covered the bed. A cherry wood dresser sat in the corner closest to the door and a roomy bedroom chair was in the opposite corner. A doorway led to an indoor water closet and Ida was duly impressed. She peeked out the window to the back gardens below. What a beautiful room.

"Do you like it?' Simon asked. "This was my room, growing up in this house. The gardens were my favorite place to explore. I'm glad Mother is putting you in here."

"It's lovely!" Ida said. "I don't know how long I will be in this room but I shall enjoy every moment of it while I am here. Is your home far?" Ida looked at the floor as she asked the question. It was a bit unnerving to be alone in a bedroom with a man— even if her sister was right downstairs.

"I live in a two-story brick house, two streets beyond my parents'. It's within walking distance but far enough to maintain my independence." Simon smiled at Ida. "I hope that you will come to love the house as your very own. I won't push you into marriage, but I do hope that we don't wait too long. I am looking forward to having you share my home."

Simon turned toward the door. "I will leave you to freshen up. There are clean towels in the water closet. The dining room is at the bottom of the stairs and to the right. I look forward to getting to know you more."

Before he left, he took her hand in his and brought it up to his lips. "You are lovelier than I ever imagined a mail-order bride could be. I am truly blessed by your response." He turned and walked out the door and back down the stairs, while Ida's eyes teared up by his caring nature.

After a delightful lunch, Elizabeth and Ida headed upstairs to rest. Simon headed back to the office with the agreement to return for breakfast. He knew the ladies needed to rest, and Harriett wanted time with Ida before he married. He hoped he could convince Ida to marry him quickly, so he could move her to his home. It was strange knowing that he now had a bride, but no wedding date. His mother had encouraged him to wait a bit before rushing Ida to the altar, but now that he had met her, his gut instinct was to marry her quickly before anything got in the way.

CHAPTER 4

A knock sounded on the door as Ida dressed for breakfast. She opened it and saw Elizabeth. "Come in. Are you ready? I was just finishing up. I didn't think it was time to go down yet."

"No, I'm a bit early. I hoped you and I would have time to talk before we headed down." Elizabeth sat on the chair in the corner, while Ida sat on the bed. "What do you think of Simon?"

Ida had tossed and turned all night as she'd thought of nothing else. Simon was easy to look at. His dark hair hung over his forehead and curled at the nape of his neck. His square-jawed face and blue eyes invaded her dreams already. "He seemed very nice. I noticed that he treats his mother with respect and was quite attentive to me."

Elizabeth smiled. "I like him. It's easier for me to imagine you married as a mail-order bride, knowing his family background. Harriett would never accept unseemly behavior toward you. Not that I imagine Simon would do that but honestly, I didn't imagine it from Stefan, other than he was very protective of you."

"Do you think Stefan will give up looking? I fear that he will track me down here in Seattle and try to take me away." Ida looked at her sister with fear in her eyes.

Elizabeth got up and sat on the bed. She reached over and hugged Ida. "I don't think that Stefan has the means to travel to Seattle, even if he figures out where you've gone. I think Bernard is planting hints that you've traveled to Wisconsin to marry a dairy farmer. If he tries to find you, he'll look there first. Now, let's go get some food."

Elizabeth and Ida went downstairs to the parlor, as the doorbell rang. Harriett looked up from her embroidery. "Fabulous timing. I was just about to come up to see if you were ready for breakfast."

Simon came into the parlor, having been let in by the maid. "Good morning, ladies. You are looking well-rested." His eyes twinkled. "I didn't think it was possible for you to look even lovelier, but here you are."

"Oh, please." Harriett said, swatting at her son. "This one is a charmer, for sure. But it's nice to see a smile on his face." She hugged him.

Max came into the parlor. "Good morning! I'm hungry, wife. Is everyone ready for some of Cynthia's fine cooking? She makes the best biscuits west of the Mississippi." He stopped and gave Harriett a kiss on the cheek.

They laughed and went into the dining room. Once breakfast was finished, they moved back into the parlor. "I was wondering," Simon said to Ida, "would you like to go to the Alaska-Yukon-Pacific Exposition today? I have heard it is a world of wonder, and there is an interesting raffle prize."

"I would love to," Ida replied, "but would we leave everyone else behind?" She was looking forward to spending time with Simon but felt guilty as she thought of leaving her sister behind.

Simon smiled. "Oh no, I was thinking that we might all

go. Father and I discussed it and made arrangements last night to surprise all of you. Later this afternoon, I'd also like to give you a tour of my home, if that's acceptable to you?"

"That sounds wonderful. Let me grab my hat and gloves from upstairs. I am so excited."

~

A SHORT WALK LATER, the five of them hopped onto a streetcar that would take them to Exposition. The streetcar was packed and Simon enjoyed the closeness of the ride. He wasn't ready to give it up when the streetcar arrived at Exposition.

Harriett and Max exited first, arm-in-arm, ready to explore. "After we talked last evening, I did a little research. There are 250 acres of ornate buildings, elaborate fountains and various exhibits. Admission is fifty cents each. We don't have to stay together but we should plan a time and location to meet around lunchtime."

Max continued, "I'd like to check out the Forestry building they constructed. It is the largest log building in existence, and I've heard it really is quite amazing. And, of course, I need to visit the Hoo-Hoo House, the log house that holds our social organization for lumbermen. Perhaps we could meet up by Geyser Basin, the big fountain, around two o'clock?"

"Sounds good," Simon said. "I would like to show Ida around the Pay Streak area. I've heard much about the attractions there."

"What is that?" Elizabeth asked.

"It is an area that includes an Eskimo village plus attractions on the Battle of Gettysburg and the Battle of the Monitor and Merrimac. There are also Native Americans, cowboys, and miners as part of the entertainment."

"Sounds exciting! I believe I'll come with you. How about you, Harriett?"

"Yes, Mother, would you like to come along?" Simon grinned at his mother and winked at Ida. He really would have preferred to be alone with his bride-to-be, but he suspected she would feel more comfortable with chaperones. He also knew his mother would like to spend time with Elizabeth since she was only here for a short period before she had to return to Beckham.

"Max and I discussed his plans this morning, and I do not think the Hoo-Hoo House is something a lady should experience." Harriett laughed. "I'd love to join you, but I think Elizabeth and I will move at our own pace. Don't let us hold you back." Harriett winked at Elizabeth and smiled.

Simon took Ida's arm in his and set off toward Pay Streak. They couldn't move too quickly along the wooden boardwalk as the crowds swelled around them vying for carnival rides and visiting the various human exhibits on display.

Ida became excited when they came upon the Gold Camps of Alaska exhibit. "Oh, may we stop and try to pan for gold? I have read that it is quite an experience."

Simon purchased two tickets to pan for gold and as they waited, they watched the raucous Wild West show. He laughed as Ida said, "Oh my word, times sure have changed, haven't they? I must admit, I wasn't sure what Seattle would be like when we boarded the train, but I am glad that it isn't as loud and untamed as the wild west appears to have been."

Ida's face was flushed with excitement, in addition to the heat in the outside exhibit. Tendrils of blonde hair curled around her face and she gazed up at him. Simon was momentarily lost for words so he smiled back. She was an angel, one that he didn't deserve. As they panned for gold in the area set up for fair-goers, he thought perhaps there was a chance that he could move ahead finally and leave his past behind him.

Next door, Harriett and Elizabeth were just coming out of the Baby Incubator Exhibit. "Oh my goodness, those tiny babies inside of those incubators. What brave little souls to face such struggles early on in life." Harriett had tears in her eyes as she spoke. "The machines are surely one of the most important discoveries of our times."

"I don't think that I shall go in," Ida stated. "I'm not sure I can handle it. What is an incubator?"

"It is a machine that creates a mechanically controlled environment for babies born too early or struggling. There were babies on display, living and breathing inside of these machines."

"Oh, dear," Ida said. "How awful for a child! I suppose the machine helps them to live and grow, but I do not wish to see that."

As the four of them walked down Pay Streak, they ooh'ed and aah'ed over the international flavor created by Chinese, Eskimo and Igorot villages. The Igorot men in their loin cloths was a bit disturbing to Ida, and Simon quickly hurried their group from the exhibit. Elizabeth liked the Streets of Cairo exhibit, which featured a camel and belly dancers although Simon was a touch embarrassed at the lack of dress.

They decided to get refreshments at a Japanese tea room and sit a spell to rest. The ladies were amazed at their afternoon tea served by beautiful Japanese women in kimonos. "This has been an unbelievable day," Ida said to Simon as they left the tea room to meet Max at the Geyser Basin fountain. "I never knew such things existed in the world or that people live in so many different environments."

"The world is unique all around us. One thing I've been told is that if our lives are not going in the right direction, we only need to change the environment around us to find a new path to follow."

Ida didn't answer him as she stopped and stared in awe. Ahead of them was the U.S. Government Building and beyond that was the Geyser Basin fountain. There was a 500 foot spillway that descended from the building, called the Cascades that flowed to the beautiful fountain. To the south, towering over the Exposition, was Mount Rainier itself, with the fresh pine trees and lingering fog hovering over Lake Union.

"What a magnificent view! This is how I imagine heaven itself would look if God were to give us a glimpse of His holy land within." Ida's eyes welled up with tears. "You're blessed to live in such a beautiful area."

Before Simon could answer, Max Farmer spotted them and came over. "How was it, ladies? I'm amazed at all they have put together. What a spectacular event! We may have to come back several times in order to see a fraction of what Exposition has to offer."

Harriett laughed. "And I suspect we will. This has been a delightful day."

～

AFTER TAKING the streetcar back to the house, and having a short bite to eat, Elizabeth said, "Would you help me upstairs with something before you leave, Ida?"

Leaving Simon and his parents in the parlor, Ida and Elizabeth went upstairs. "What did you wish to speak to me about?"

"I'd like you to discuss with Simon when your wedding ceremony will take place." Elizabeth said, smiling gently. "Don't shake your head at me. You came here to marry him, and I'd like to attend your wedding before I leave."

"But how can I be certain of his character? How can I know that he will never hurt me?"

"He seems like a fine man. I haven't seen any signs of any ungentlemanly behaviors. I'm certain that Harriett, who supports battered and abused women, would never allow her son to be anything but caring toward his spouse."

Elizabeth reached over and gave Ida a hug. "I cannot guarantee that he will never be disagreeable. Marriage comes with challenges that each of us must work through. Bernard and I have had many fights, but we love each other and we work together to find a common goal. Communication and trust are the two most important things in a marriage. You'll learn to trust him, but you must give it time."

Ida sighed. "I know you're right, my head says you are. The rest of me, however, is scared beyond belief that Simon is not who you believe him to be. At the same time, what if Stefan finds me and forces me to marry him. I could not survive such a situation."

"Trust me and trust Harriett. You'll be marrying into a good family and be in good hands. If something does go wrong, and you find yourself in a bad situation, don't stay. Get out. Contact me, and Bernard will come get you immediately. Whatever it takes."

Ida took a deep breath. "Does every bride get this speech, or is it just me because of my situation?" She was starting to feel like a child being scolded by her mother. However, the memory of Stefan's hands on her and the sting of the bruises helped her defend her thoughts. Surviving abuse was not a sign of weakness, and she would enter this relationship with her eyes open and her head clear.

Elizabeth shrugged and took Ida's hands in hers. "Every bride I match gets this treatment. No person should stay in a situation that is physically abusive, emotionally demeaning, or verbally critical. Never be afraid to leave." She pulled Ida into a hug. "I love you. I hate what Stefan has done to you. I wish you nothing but happiness and joy for the rest of your life. Trust Simon."

Ida pulled out of the hug and walked over to the window. The midday sun shone brightly on the busy street below. "Saturday. Do you think Saturday would be too soon? I will talk to Simon tonight."

"I think that would be perfect. It gives us five days to plan the wedding. My train back to Beckham leaves Sunday, and if I'm not on it, Bernard has promised to travel to Seattle himself and throw me over his shoulder to drag me home." Elizabeth and Ida laughed at the idea of Bernard's threats. They both knew Elizabeth had Bernard wrapped around her little finger and the adoration was mutual. "Now, let's head back downstairs so you can visit your soon-to-be new home."

Simon and Ida stepped outside, and Simon helped her into the carriage. Waving good-bye to Elizabeth and his parents, Simon asked, "Would you like the direct route or the scenic tour?"

"Oh, the scenic route please. This city is so lovely, I'd like to see more of it." In truth, Ida was a bit nervous to go directly to his home and hoped to put it off for a bit longer.

As Simon drove the carriage along Madison Street from Fourth Avenue to Broadway, Ida commented, "This is a lovely drive. The trees are majestic and appear to climb to heaven. I don't believe I've seen them in Beckham. What kind of tree are these?"

Simon noted, "Lombardy poplar trees. This is one of the most beautiful drives in town. The trees are a favorite attraction for many of us in Seattle."

Ida gazed in awe at the stately trees. "I can see why. This drive is relaxing. I feel as if I am in the country and not in Seattle at all."

Simon laughed. "On your left is The Central School, which houses Seattle's high school. The Knickerbocker Hotel is on the right, built for Exposition, and extremely modern. I have heard apartments there have a weekly rate of $3.00 but many residents enjoy the close proximity it has to downtown entertainment."

"I am amazed at the hustle and bustle around town. There is such modernization and so many people here." Ida looked around curiously. "Do you work near here?"

"My office is not far. It is a few blocks away near the new municipal building on Yesler Way." Simon appreciated her interest in his work. "Seattle has experienced much growth in the past few years. Will it bother you to live in the city or would you prefer a country setting?"

"Oh goodness, no! I find this fast-pace quite exciting. I think I like how a person can get lost in the crowd here...and never be found by those looking for them." Ida said the last part quietly but Simon heard her. He glanced over at her and noticed tears in her eyes.

"I don't mean to pry, but is there something in your past that you are running from?" Simon stopped the carriage on the side of the road. He took Ida's hand in his, while his thumb stroked the top of her hand. "Look at me," he said, as he used his other hand to tilt her chin up. Her eyes filled with tears even more.

"You are safe here. I will protect you, and I will never hurt you. I don't know what you're running from, but I know what you have run to. You have come to me and as my wife, I will lay down my life to protect you. Even though we have yet to set a date to say these words, please know that I will stand by you for better or for worse, for richer or poorer, through sickness or in health. I will cherish you from this day forward until death parts us, even if the marriage is in name only."

He let go of her chin and wiped the tears off her face with his thumb. Ida forced a smile and replied, "I promise to tell you more at a later time when we're not on the street, but for now, it's time to tour your lovely home."

Simon squeezed her hand and let go of it, as he gently cupped her right cheek. "And soon to be your home. We have much to learn about each other. I look forward to sharing the ghosts of our pasts." He started the carriage again and continued on.

After a few more turns, they stopped in front of a two-story red brick home. Simon came around to help her out of the carriage. He reached up and put his hands around her waist as he helped her down. Ida placed her hands on his shoulders. Their faces were mere inches apart and Ida could smell a hint of mint coming from Simon. He paused and they gazed into each other's eyes. Being the gentleman that he was, Simon released her waist and led her into his home.

As he opened the door, Simon said, "Mrs. Picklebottom? I'm home."

Ida giggled and whispered, "Mrs. Picklebottom? What a funny name."

Simon smiled. "She is my housekeeper and cook combined. She comes several times a week to help clean. I told her I was bringing you to visit today and she insisted on coming while I was out to tidy up the place." Simon sighed.

An older woman, slightly smaller than five feet tall and almost as round as she was tall, shuffled slowly down the hallway to the right. She had snow white curly hair, eyes that twinkled mischievously and an infectious smile. She came over and gave Ida a big hug. Ida couldn't help feeling like she might tell this woman anything and she would understand.

"You must be Miss Ida. Welcome, welcome! I think you will bring much happiness and sunshine back into Simon's life." She smiled brightly at Simon as she spoke. "I am Mrs.

Picklebottom. Simon has told me much about your coming. I hope you had a wonderful day at the Exposition."

"I am delighted to meet you, Mrs. Picklebottom. Do you live here with Simon?"

"Oh no, dearie, I live around the corner with my daughter and her family. Simon provides me a place when I need to escape the craziness of living with a family of eight." Mrs. Picklebottom patted Simon on his right cheek. "I come several times a week to help clean and cook a few meals to make sure this boy still has meat on his bones. If he had to rely on his own cooking, I'm afraid he might waste away." She laughed heartily at her own joke.

"All right now, no more giving away my secrets, Mrs. Picklebottom. I'm going to give Ida a quick tour. Do you think we might talk you into sharing some of your sweet lemonade with us?" Simon winked at Ida over Mrs. Picklebottom's head. "We'll be back to the front parlor shortly, so the two of us can talk and become better acquainted."

"Absolutely, I made it this morning and have been keeping it cool in the icebox for you. I'd be tickled for you to try it, Miss Ida, and let me know what you think." She waddled back toward the kitchen to prepare the refreshments.

Simon showed Ida around the first floor of the home. To the right of the front door was a dining room with a beautiful oak table and eight chairs. "This table is lovely, Simon. Where did you find it?" Ida said, running her hand over the smooth wood.

"My father actually made it by hand. In addition to cutting the trees down, he occasionally makes furniture in his spare time. He says he likes to escape from mother, but I think it relaxes him. I've never seen them exchange a harsh word."

Behind the dining room was the kitchen, which they

passed as to not disturb Mrs. Picklebottom in her lemonade preparation, a water closet, and a sitting room. The sitting room included a walnut writing table, several bookcases filled with books, and a sofa. Near the back window, a small table separated two soft chairs that overlooked the back yard.

"Oh, I could sit here all day and read a book. What a magnificent space and view this is!"

Simon chuckled. "This room is my favorite room in the house. I spend much time here ruminating on the day's events and life's challenges."

They headed back to the left of the front door, where the parlor was. "There are three bedrooms upstairs and a second water closet. However, I think I will save those for another day."

As they entered the parlor, Ida noticed a square rosewood piano in the front corner, near the window. In the center of the room was a fireplace, surrounded by two large uphol-stered rosewood sofas, two large chairs and several smaller chairs covered in the same material. A marble-topped mahogany table was placed next to each of the two large chairs.

Simon and Ida each sat in a large chair across from the other as Mrs. Picklebottom shuffled in with the lemonade and a tray of cookies. "Here you go, dearies. I'm off to prepare dinner for my family. Is there anything else you need before I go?"

"No thank you," Simon said. "Will I see you tomorrow at the usual time?"

"Absolutely! It was nice meeting you, Ida. I can't wait to get to know you better."

"Thank you, Mrs. Picklebottom. You have a lovely evening and perhaps we shall run into each other tomorrow as well."

Mrs. Picklebottom gathered her things and slipped out

the front door with a cheery goodbye. Simon and Ida were left alone in the parlor.

Ida looked around nervously. It felt safe when someone else was here but now that she was alone with Simon, she wasn't sure how to feel. Part of her wanted to sit with him on the sofa and feel his body next to hers. The other part of her wanted to run to safety. Being near him brought her such confusion. She glanced over at him. His dark hair hung over his forehead, and she fought the urge to lean over and swipe it back from his face. His blue eyes looked intently at her, as he caught her staring.

"Ida..." Simon began. This was not going to be an easy conversation. "I wondered if we might talk about the wedding. I'd like to marry you as soon as you are ready. I know we haven't known each other that long but I'm ready to take each day as it comes."

Ida knew this conversation was coming. "Elizabeth and I were talking about it this morning. I think that I will be ready by Saturday."

"I suppose five days isn't too long to wait. I'd like to get to know you better before we walk down that aisle." Simon approached the topic gently. He softly spoke, "Do you think you might tell me what it is you are running from? I'd like to help."

Ida turned her face toward the window and looked outside. She wondered what would be the best approach to sharing her story. A knock on the door saved her from answering.

Simon got up to answer the door as Ida stood to follow. "Mother?"

"Elizabeth?" Ida said. She looked at her sister's face. "What's wrong?"

Both women rushed into the house. "Shut the door, Simon. Quickly!" Harriett urged him.

"What is going on?" Simon shut the door quickly and turned to her.

"A man came by our house today. He was looking for Ida."

Elizabeth turned to Ida. "It was Stefan."

Ida's face turned pale and she slid to the floor. As she came to, she felt herself being lifted into Simon's arms. His solid chest and the beat of his heart felt comforting. He carried her to one of the sofas and lay her down.

"Ida?" he said softly. "Ida, honey, are you all right?" He fanned her face with his hand.

"I'm…I'm fine. Help me sit up, please."

Simon helped her sit up and then sat on the sofa next to her. He placed his left arm around her shoulders.

Elizabeth and Harriett sat in the two large chairs. Elizabeth was wringing her hands and repeating, "I'm sorry. I don't think he saw me but he looked around suspiciously before he left. I'm so sorry."

"Please stop, Elizabeth, it's not your fault. I wonder how he found me." Ida's eyes were filled with tears and she shook with fear.

"Don't you worry, we'll do whatever we need to do to protect you." Harriett said. "I'll hide you in the women's shelter if I have to. He won't be able to get you there."

Simon was thoroughly confused as to what was going on. The women continued to chatter around him. He interrupted loudly, "Could you please stop?" All three women stopped talking and stared at him. "Would someone please tell me what is going on?" he demanded. "Who is Stefan? And why is he looking for Ida?"

Elizabeth started to speak, but Ida stopped her with a wave of her hand. "This is my story, Elizabeth. He deserves to know. I'll tell him."

"Stefan is, or was, my fiancé. We were together for nine months. At first, he was kind and generous to a fault. He bought me gifts and took me to the theater and local restaurants. Over time, however, he began to control my life. It got progressively worse as time went on. He told me who I could or couldn't see. He began to criticize what I wore, and I could do nothing right. About three months into the relationship, he began to strike out at me." Ida cried as she told the story, tears streaming down her face. "One time I accidently spilled coffee on him. He grabbed my wrist and twisted it harshly behind my back. He told me if I ever did it again that he would kill me. He followed me to the store and on several occasions, he would trip me as I went by, causing me to stumble against things. I had bruises that covered several areas of my body at all times. He wouldn't allow me to escape or leave, so I went to Elizabeth under the cloak of darkness when he thought I was in for the evening."

Simon got up off the sofa and walked over to the window. He stared outside, taking a moment to think.

Elizabeth looked at Ida, with tears in her eyes. "I couldn't say no to my youngest sister. I wouldn't say no to any woman who needed help. I hid her in my house and told Stefan that she wasn't there. He's been searching for her ever since. Unfortunately, despite our best efforts, it looks like he's found her."

Ida wiped her eyes. "I won't go with him. I'm sorry I answered your letter without being truthful, Simon. I needed to escape Beckham. When I read your letter, it spoke to my heart. I felt that if anyone would understand my predicament, it would be you. Your compassionate words touched me in a place that nothing has before. I felt as if God was leading me to you and I'm sorry if I've hurt you."

Simon turned and walked back to the sofa. "I have felt a connection with you since you have arrived. I haven't felt that way about another person in the past three years. I knew something was off and you were hiding something from me.

I wish you would have been honest with me before now but I do understand why you didn't."

"I'm sorry, Simon, I truly am. I didn't know how to tell you. I almost told you on the ride over here but it didn't feel right."

"There's only one thing I can do. I can't think of any other options." Simon stood up.

"Simon Farmer, you cannot abandon this girl…" Harriett began but Simon interrupted her.

"Not now," he said. He got down on one knee and took Ida's hand in his. "Ida Mae Miller, would you do me the great honor of becoming my wife? Not Saturday, but tomorrow? The time I have spent with you has taught me how to laugh again. I know that we have much to learn about each other, but I'd like to be by your side as we discover all those surprises that God has in store for us."

Elizabeth covered her mouth with her hand. Harriett smiled with tears in her eyes. Ida slid off the sofa onto the floor on her knees and took Simon's hands in hers. "I would be honored to become your wife. I can see a gentleness in your character that doesn't exist in people like Stefan. You have a wonderful family that supports you and cares about you a great deal. If we are married, Stefan cannot touch me. I am humbled by your thoughtfulness and I accept."

Elizabeth and Harriett jumped up off the chairs and hugged each other. "Oh my goodness, we have so much to do." Harriett shrieked. "I'll contact Pastor Roberts and ask him if he is available. Will a backyard wedding be acceptable?"

"That sounds perfect. Ida can stay here tonight and get ready in one of the bedrooms upstairs tomorrow."

"I understand the need to keep her safe," Elizabeth said, "but I'd like to stay with her here tonight, if you don't mind."

Ida nodded, relieved. "Yes, I'd like that very much. Could Elizabeth stay with me?"

"Of course," Simon said. "I want you to feel comfortable and safe. Elizabeth would be a great help to you tomorrow as you prepare for the wedding."

"I'd also like to bake a cake," Elizabeth said. "Do you have the supplies?"

"I'm sure Mrs. Picklebottom has all the supplies that you need. I'll show you to the kitchen and get you both settled."

Harriett hugged Simon and said, "I'll bring over your dress in the morning, Ida. It's hanging in the closet upstairs?" Ida nodded and Harriett rushed home. She promised to send Max back with an overnight bag before he tracked down Pastor Roberts.

Simon locked the front door behind his mother and turned with a smile. "Are you ready to see the kitchen, ladies, before I give you the tour of the upstairs?"

The kitchen was near the back of the house behind the dining room. It was a fairly small and simple kitchen. There was a cast iron stove against the outer wall. Opposite to that was a sink with a counter on either side. In the center of the room stood a small wooden table. A free-standing cupboard was near the sink and an ironing board was in one corner of the room. Near the stove was a rocking chair. A door from the kitchen led to a back porch where the icebox was located, as well as the gardens behind the house.

"This is a perfect workroom." Elizabeth said as Ida nodded. "How many days a week does Mrs. Picklebottom come in to help?"

"Right now, she comes in two days a week and an occasional third day, if needed. The other days she spends at home with her daughter's family."

Ida opened a door off to the right near the back porch and found a small pantry. "Oh, this is perfect. All the supplies needed for a cake are right here. I do hope you let me know what your favorite foods are, so I can make them for you."

Simon chuckled. "Oh, no worries, there. I suspect I'll like whatever you cook. Mrs. Picklebottom will tell you that I can't survive on my own merits in that area. But if I'm hankering for something in particular, I'll be glad to let you know."

Ida found that she liked his deep chuckle. It warmed her insides like a cup of hot cocoa or a small piece of chocolate. She knew she could listen to his rich voice all day and laugh together as they relaxed in the lovely sitting room, reading books. She could imagine a little girl with her blonde curls curled up in his lap, as Simon read a story while she knitted a blanket during the cold winter months.

A knock at the front door interrupted their tour. Simon left the ladies in the kitchen while he answered it. He came back fairly quickly. "Father dropped off an overnight bag for each of you. Would you like to see your rooms?"

"Yes, please," Ida said as she covered a yawn. "It is getting late, and it's been a long day."

The three of them went upstairs to the bedrooms. Simon carried both bags up the stairs. Simon showed them the water closet, located at the top of the stairs and led them to the two additional bedrooms on the right.

"These bedrooms are connected. There is a walk-in closet between the two rooms as well. You will each have your own room but be connected as well. Will that work for you?" Simon looked at Ida as he talked. He was concerned that she wouldn't be comfortable with how fast things were moving.

Completely overwhelmed, Ida nodded shyly at Simon and took a deep breath. This was all happening so quickly. "That sounds fine, thank you."

Simon left the bags with the ladies and went back downstairs to the sitting room. Elizabeth sat on the bed with Ida after he left.

"This is a lovely room." Elizabeth said, as she sat on the bed. "I'm sure you're nervous for tomorrow. Do you have any questions for me?"

Ida walked over to the window and looked outside at the street below. "Yes, why is he here?" she replied angrily. "Why did Stefan have to follow me?" She turned and walked over to the bed. Ida felt warm, thick tears start to fall on her cheeks. "Why? That's my question. Why?" She put her face in her hands and started to sob.

Elizabeth pulled her close and let her cry, as she rubbed her back. "It's ok, sweetie, it's ok. Let it out."

Elizabeth let Ida cry it out until her sobs subsided. "Are you sure you want to go through with this? It's not too late to change your mind."

Ida took a deep breath. "No, I don't want to change my mind. I find Simon very attractive, and I think he feels the same. It's just happening so quickly. And I'm angry at Stefan for interfering in my life."

"I know and you will rise above this. In the meantime, let me tell you about the marriage bed." Elizabeth wiggled her eyebrows and Ida laughed.

A half hour later, Ida lay in bed going over in her head what Elizabeth had shared with her. She closed her eyes, he was so handsome. Never in her wildest dreams had she imagined a man like that would ever look in her direction. She could love him forever. Love? She wasn't in love. Her skin tingled as she thought of his touch, his hand in hers, his broad chest holding her tightly. He was every inch a man but they had only just met. Tossing and turning, she tried her best to fall asleep. Once she did, she dreamed of a dark shadow chasing her, and a gentle hand caressing her face, stroking her arm gently, whispering to her to trust him.

CHAPTER 5

*T*he next morning, Ida awoke to the smell of bacon and eggs and coffee. Oh, Lord, hot coffee – that was enough to settle any nerves she might have. Elizabeth came in with a tray and set it down on the table next to the bed.

"Wake up, sleepy head! I let you sleep in this morning since I thought you probably needed the rest. But, I've heard Pastor Roberts will be here for a noon wedding so it's time to roll out of bed and prepare for the day!"

After a delicious breakfast, Ida decided to bathe. She closed her eyes in the tub and reflected on her future. She'd seen the way Simon looked at her, and her body tingled at the thought. She realized that tonight she would be home alone with him. Would he expect her to share his bed? Was she ready for that? She would be his wife, but they had just met. Maybe he would be kind enough to give her some time before she would need to fulfill that role. Or maybe she should just share his bed and lie there until he was finished?

She finished bathing and walked back into the bedroom to get dressed. As she was combing through her hair, Elizabeth came through the walk-in closet, carrying a dress. "Knock, knock, I'm coming in. Harriett sent over her maid, Cynthia, with this." She placed the dress on the bed and sat down. As Ida combed her hair, Elizabeth asked, "Would you like me to style it for you?"

"I would love that." Ida sat down on the bed next to Elizabeth. "Are you sure Stefan isn't lurking around outside? I am scared at the thought of what he might do."

Elizabeth hugged her. "I don't think he is. But that's why we're having the wedding in the back yard. He doesn't have access to the gardens. Harriett told me that there is a six-foot brick wall surrounding the back gardens. We couldn't hope for a more private location."

"How are the arrangements? Is everything almost ready?" Ida asked. "I'm so nervous, I could throw up. Am I doing the right thing?"

"I think you are. Just take one day at a time and trust your heart. God will not lead you in a direction away from Him. You just have to listen closely." Elizabeth braided Ida's hair into a crown around her head as she spoke. Her remaining blonde hair fell loosely down the back of her neck. "Remember, also, that marriage involves two different people. There will be challenges and frustrations that come up. The two of you will need to learn to communicate and work together to solve your differences."

Elizabeth stood up and held out the mirror to Ida. "You look beautiful. I'm going to let you get dressed now while I go downstairs to make sure the pastor is here. Simon is outside, so you can come down when you're ready." She kissed Ida on the check and left the room.

Ida got dressed and took a deep breath. She left the room to head downstairs when she noticed the master bedroom door was open. She quickly peeked inside. A large bed stood in the center of the room, a beautiful Pine Burr quilt lay on the bed. A light blue border played against the pink and green shapes on the quilt. It was a uniquely handmade masterpiece, lovingly crafted to ensure warmth on a cold Seattle evening. Ida had never seen anything quite like it.

The bedroom had a large window overlooking Seattle. A sturdy five-drawer dresser was in the corner, along with a nightstand on either side of the bed. Everything was neat and tidy in the room from what she could see. The room definitely needed a woman's touch but her eyes were drawn back to the quilt. A female hand had definitely made that. Perhaps Simon had received it as a gift.

Hearing voices below, she backed out of the room and descended the stairs. Max Farmer was standing at the bottom. "You look lovely. I was coming to see if you would like an escort down the aisle."

"Thank you, Max. I would love for you to give me away."

He stepped outside to tell everyone that the wedding was about to begin. Elizabeth and Harriett took their seats along with Mrs. Picklebottom. Simon's younger brother and two youngest sisters were in attendance, as were his Aunt Mary and Uncle Fred. Harriett had lined up a violinist to play the procession, and as she began to play, Max went back inside to collect Ida.

Ida and Max stepped outside and slowly marched down the short path to the hastily thrown together altar. Ida clung to Max's arm and kept her eyes on Simon. He looked dashedly handsome in a gray suit and maroon tie. His eyes peered into the depths of her soul and a calmness filled her being. She focused on him and nothing else.

Simon watched the vision that was coming toward him down the aisle. Her blonde hair glowed in the sunlight, and a smile was pasted on her face. She looked petrified and she clung to his father's arm. Her blue eyes, however, looked into his as she walked, and he could see strength and courage there. He wished he could reassure her that all would be fine, but they didn't have the time to talk. He tried to convey that message through his eyes as he looked at her.

As they reached the end of the aisle, Max placed her hand into Simon's. Pastor Roberts asked, "Who gives this woman in marriage?"

"Well, Harriett and I do and her sister, Elizabeth, I guess."

Pastor Roberts began the ceremony and Simon stroked the top of her hand with his thumb. She tried to focus on the words that were being said, but the sensation of his hand on hers filled her body with heat. 'Focus, Ida, Focus,' she said to herself.

"I ask each of you now, to repeat the marriage vows after me." Pastor Roberts was speaking, so Ida focused in on his voice. "I, Simon, take you, Ida, for my wedded wife."

Simon repeated the words. "I, Simon, take you, Debra…"

Ida blinked. *What did he say?* Did she hear him correctly? Nobody said a word.

His voice stumbled, "…um, take you, Ida, for my wedded wife."

The rest of the ceremony passed in a blur. Ida didn't remember stating her vows or saying 'I do' but she knew she must have when Pastor Roberts said, "I now pronounce you husband and wife. You may kiss the bride."

Simon put his hand under chin and tilted her face up for their first kiss. When his lips softly touched hers, she felt a tingling from the tips of her toes to the top of her head. It felt like every fiber of her body was on fire. She had never felt anything like this before. She forgot her brief confusion and focused on how alive his kiss made her feel. Unfortunately, it was over too quickly and Simon released her. She already missed the feel of his lips on hers and he looked as glassy-eyed as she.

As they turned to face the crowd, Ida quickly remembered Simon's error. Max and Harriett were giving Simon a strange look and Elizabeth was looking at her with compassion. Mrs. Picklebottom was sobbing and blowing her nose into her handkerchief. Ida pasted a false smile on her face and walked down the aisle with Simon. She and her new husband would have a little talk once her new family and sister left.

~

A CELEBRATION FOLLOWED INSIDE, which included a potluck of various dishes well-wishers had brought, and Ida met the rest of Simon's family. She enjoyed the conversation and pushed the wedding blunder into the back of her mind. However, it was soon time for people to leave and return home. After a whispered conversation with his parents, Simon thanked Pastor Roberts for coming on such short notice to perform the ceremony.

"Always glad to help out a parishioner, lad. Particularly one with such understanding parents willing to pay handsomely for last minute services." Pastor Roberts winked at Simon. "I hope to see you and your lovely new bride at church service on Sunday."

"Yes, sir. I look forward to introducing Ida to the women of the congregation. I suspect my new bride will want to jump right in and make new friends." Simon looked worriedly over his shoulder at Ida. She stood in the corner of the parlor next to the piano, glancing over at him, while talking to Elizabeth and wringing her hands. When she saw him looking, she quickly looked away.

Simon jumped when Pastor Roberts placed a hand on his shoulder. "She's worth the effort, son. Talk to her about the past and you may find that forgiveness is but a small step away." Pastor Roberts looked compassionately at him. "Jesus taught us that it is necessary to forgive seventy-seven times. I suspect that number may be higher in married life." Pastor Roberts laughed and waved as he stepped out the door.

In the corner, Ida was beside herself. "You heard him, he called me Debra. Who is Debra?" She was in tears and Elizabeth was trying to soothe her.

"I know it looks bad, but you need to ask Simon that question." Elizabeth and Harriett had talked about Simon's past earlier, when Ida had left with Simon to tour the house. But it wasn't her story to tell. "You both have a past and the two of you haven't had time to talk about what brought you together.

"Every letter that comes into the agency from a potential groom comes with a story. Every bride that answers those letters has a background of her own. I don't know the history of each person, but I know that each couple I connect will most likely have issues and face trials together. That's what marriage is and it's how it grows. Unfortunately, with a mail order couple, the relationship is built after the marriage, and it holds its own set of unique challenges." Elizabeth hugged her sister. "I think you're up to the challenge. Talk to him. He's been through a lot as well."

Elizabeth, Harriett and Max said their good-byes and promised to be on the lookout for Stefan. As they stepped out the door, Ida went back into the parlor and sat down. A few moments later, Simon joined her and sat next to her on the sofa. He wasn't sure what to say but he knew it was his fault. It was just his luck that she would have heard his wedding blunder. He shook his head, he was such an idiot!

"Ida? You're awfully quiet. It's all my fault. Is there anything I can do?"

Ida turned and looked directly at him. Her blue eyes were dark and he could see the thunderclouds inside them. Oh, this was not going to be easy.

"Really? Are you really going to ask me that, Simon?" Ida felt her anger bubble and burst. "Why don't you start by telling me what's going on?" She felt the heat inside her rise and she stood to pace the room. "I travelled seven days to get here. I've been followed by a monster who won't let me be. I met a man whose touch makes my thoughts become jumbled. I rushed into a marriage, anticipating that it could be something dreams are made of and now?"

Ida stopped pacing and turned to Simon with warm tears streaming down her face. "Now that I've survived all that, I have to wonder, who is Debra?" She sat on the couch and buried her face in her hands.

Simon felt like a heel. This mail-order bride situation wasn't turning out at all like he had imagined. When did life get so complicated?

He took a deep breath. "You've told me your background. I suppose it's only fair to tell you mine. Debra was my fiancée. We met at the university and fell in love. After graduation, John Gorvin, her father, hired me to work for him in his law firm in San Francisco. Three years ago, we were planning our wedding when things went horribly wrong." Simon ran his hand through his hair.

Ida raised her eyes and looked at him "What happened? Did she leave you?"

His eyes filled with tears. "That would actually have been easier. I told you in my letter that my past is filled with nightmares of memories I cannot change. On April eighteenth, three years ago, San Francisco experienced an earthquake of epic proportions. I'm sure you've heard of it. Eighty percent of the city was destroyed." His eyes took on a haunted look as he relived the horror in his mind to tell the tale.

"Debra was home in bed, as were her parents. It was a little after five in the morning. The earthquake destroyed their home. Her mother was killed instantly. Her father, John, was pierced by a falling beam. Debra was trapped by debris."

Ida looked at him in horror. "Those poor souls. How awful!"

Simon kept talking, not hearing her. "I rushed over to their house on Hayes Street as quickly as I could. By then though, the fire had started. A woman had been making breakfast for her family when the quake hit. It accidently started the 'Ham and Eggs Fire'. The fire spread to surrounding houses very quickly. It burned out of control, and I couldn't get to her."

Simon's anguish was horrific, and Ida reached out to him and held him. He cried, "I tried. I tried to get to her, to save her, but the firefighters wouldn't let me inside. They pushed me back and insisted I leave. By the time the fire was out, she was gone." Simon sat back and took a deep breath. "All I have left of her is a quilt that she made me. It is on my bed to remind me of her love for me."

Ida didn't know what to say to that, so she remained silent.

"I have spent the years since trying to outrun my sorrows. I am ready to learn to live again, with you, but I fear I have wronged you. I am so sorry. I wish I could turn back time and correct my blunder."

Ida took his hand. "I am so very sorry for your loss. I had no idea what you had gone through. I wish I had known. We've both experienced broken hearts and perhaps together, we can heal."

Ida rested her head on Simon's shoulder as they sat there holding hands. Both of them were drained of energy after all that had happened. Simon rubbed his thumb along hers. After a few minutes, Simon said quietly, "Ida?"

"Yes?" She enjoyed sitting so close to him, relaxing together.

"May I kiss you?"

She turned her head and looked up at him, as she nodded. Simon brought his head closer and softly brushed his lips over hers. A shock went through her body at his touch. His hand stroked down her side, moving to her back and pulling her closer against him. His tongue probed at her lips, asking for permission to enter.

She let out a low moan and parted her lips, granting him access. She put her hands behind his head and put her fingers into the dark hair at the nape of his neck. She certainly liked his kisses. "Your lips are so soft," Simon mumbled, as he ended it.

Ida was out of breath and felt overheated as he finally broke off the kiss. Looking into his blue eyes, she said, "I don't think this is a good idea."

"Why not? We're married. It's what married couples do."

"I'm not ready to share your bed," she stated. "Or your quilt," she muttered under her breath, then said a bit louder, "I was hoping that we could have some time to get to know each other better."

"How long do you need?" Simon looked warily at her. He wasn't surprised at her request but he had been hoping the intimacy would bring them closer together and chase away the demons of his past.

"A week? I'm not really sure. I just feel like I'll know when it's time." Ida hated asking him to wait, but she felt uncomfortable rushing into relations so quickly. He was virtually a stranger, even though he was also her handsome husband.

Simon stood. "May I walk you to your room, mi'lady?" He held out his arm.

Ida accepted his arm and giggled. "Absolutely, my lord."

He led her upstairs and to the room she had slept in the previous evening.

He hovered in the doorway for a moment, before saying, "I'll leave you to it, then. Good night, wife."

"Good night, husband." Ida shut the door behind him. She leaned back against the door for a moment. Tears fell from her face. Her husband was in love with the ghost of his deceased fiancée, her ex-fiancé was in Seattle trying to find her, her sister was leaving shortly to return to Beckham, and everyone she knew lived on the other side of the country. She felt tears streaming down her face and walked over to the bed. As she threw herself onto the mattress, and buried her face in the pillows, allowing the sobs to overcome her, she wondered what on earth she had done.

CHAPTER 6

The next morning, Ida awoke bright and early.
Getting out of bed, she hurried to the bathroom.
After washing, she got dressed and went downstairs. She
found an apron hanging on the back of the door. After
putting it on, she got bacon out of the ice box and carefully
sliced off long strips to fry. She gathered eggs in a bowl and
scrambled them together with a little milk, a hint of butter,
and a dash of pepper. She couldn't find any bread for toast
and added that to her list of things to do today. She made a
pot of coffee for Simon and heated water for tea for herself.

Ida was putting breakfast on the table when Simon came
downstairs. He looked surprised to see the meal before him.
"Good morning," he said apprehensively, as he came over and
kissed her on the cheek.

"Good morning! I was afraid that I might have to come
upstairs and wake you." Ida teased.

Simon chuckled. "It's not every day a man gets married.
He should be able to sleep in after his wedding night." He
stopped chuckling when Ida didn't respond. "Ida? Are you all
right?"

"I'm sorry," she said. "It wasn't much of a wedding night. It's all my fault." She wrung her hands in the apron.

"Sit down, please." Simon sat across the table from her. "If anything, it's my fault. I made a mess out of our wedding vows. I didn't take the time to tell you about Debra before we married." He took a deep breath. "And I haven't told you yet how beautiful and absolutely charming I find you."

She looked up at him, confused. "What do you mean?"

"I admit my world was destroyed three years ago. Losing Debra meant losing all that I had worked for and built." Simon looked at her with a sad look in his eyes. "You are my world now. You are the woman I want to build a future with. Can you believe me?"

Ida nodded, not trusting herself to speak. If this was a dream, she wasn't ready to awaken.

"I will spend the rest of my life courting you and making you believe that. Now, let's pray, shall we?" Simon said the prayer for them before serving himself a heaping spoonful of the eggs and several slices of bacon. He took a bite of eggs and closed his eyes as he savored the taste. He heaved a huge sigh.

"What is it, what's wrong?" Ida asked. She knew she was a good cook, so he couldn't be disappointed in the taste of the eggs. She might be a horrible wife, but she could definitely keep him well fed.

"These are the best scrambled eggs I've ever tasted." Simon grinned and took a bite of his bacon. "And the most delicious bacon too."

Ida smiled. There wasn't anything special to the meal. "Let me ask you a question. Are you used to making your own breakfast?"

Simon laughed loudly. "Why, yes, I am. I usually make a pot of coffee and eat a slice of toast. I don't cook much. How did you know?"

Ida giggled. "I've never seen anyone enjoy bacon and eggs quite as much."

"If you keep cooking like this every morning, I might have to buy my clothes a little larger." Simon patted his stomach, as he grabbed a few more slices of bacon.

"What are your plans for the day?" Ida asked, after Simon finished the last bite.

"I have to go into the office this morning to work on a few cases," Simon sighed. "I wish I could stay and spend the morning with you, but this work can't be put off. I could come home a little early though. Would you like to take a walk and go to dinner afterwards?"

"That sounds lovely. I'll spend some time doing the wash and getting some baking done. I'd like to make a couple of loaves of fresh bread." Ida thought for a moment. "Will Mrs. Picklebottom be coming by today?"

"No, I talked to her yesterday. Her normal days are Thursday and Saturday. On occasion, she picks a third day to come by and make sure all is well. Since she was here to meet you earlier this week, I expect she'll be back on Thursday."

Simon stood. "That was delicious. Thank you for making me breakfast. I'll see you around three o'clock." He walked over to the door, grabbed his hat and disappeared before she could say anything else.

She collected the breakfast dishes and carried them to the kitchen sink, scrubbing what she'd used that morning. After she finished that task, she mixed up several loaves of bread, dividing the bread dough into three individual pans and covered them with a towel while she washed the dining room table and scrubbed the floor. Once the dining room was spotless, she put the bread into the oven to bake.

She went into the sitting room and decided a thorough cleaning was in order. She wiped down the mahogany table and dusted the bookshelves. There were several books to be put away and she quickly learned Simon's filing system. This was such a beautiful room, she could see why it was Simon's favorite. She sat in one of the soft chairs and gazed out the window into the back yard. It seemed like only yesterday that she'd boarded the train to come to Seattle. A giant willow tree provided shade and the branches moved slightly with the gentle wind that was blowing. Ida smiled and closed her eyes for a moment as she soaked in the beauty of the day.

The smell of fresh bread brought her to her senses quickly, and she hopped out of the chair and hurried into the kitchen. She took the bread out of the oven and smiled as she saw how perfectly the loaves had come out. Setting the loaves on the table, she used a tiny bit of butter to brush over the top of each loaf. Then she covered them with a cloth and left them to cool.

She went upstairs and tidied the guest room she slept in. She wasn't sure how many nights she would spend in the room, but she wanted to make sure everything was as she had found it. Her wedding dress hung in the closet along with her other dresses. She swept the wooden floors of both guest rooms with the broom from the upstairs closet and dusted the dressers.

By the time Simon came home later that afternoon, the upstairs bedrooms and downstairs areas were sparkling clean. Ida was sitting on the sofa, crocheting a blanket with yarn she had brought with her from Beckham. It was her favorite pastime and helped her relax. She wasn't sure exactly what time Simon was going to be home, and she wasn't ready to help herself to a book from his small library in the sitting room without asking him first.

Simon came in and kissed her on the cheek. "You've been busy," he said, looking around the room and noticing the shine. "What are you making?"

"I thought that I would crochet some blankets for the

winter months. Perhaps Harriett could use them at the battered women's shelter, so the women there know that they are not alone. There are others who understand what they have gone through."

"I am proud of you." Simon sat down next to Ida on the sofa. "From what you've shared with me, I know that you are a woman full of strength and courage. You recognized the danger of a future with Stefan and you acted on that wisdom to escape. Not every woman would have the insight or the mettle to do so."

"Thank you for saying so. I don't feel brave. I feel like a tumbleweed blowing in the wind, trying to turn myself away from Stefan's path."

"Well, you're here now, and I will protect you from him if he comes back." Simon promised her. "Now, are you ready to go for that walk I promised earlier?"

"I would love it." Ida said. "Should I pack something quickly for a picnic afterwards?"

"No, I'd like to take you out for a taste of Seattle's seafood tonight. It is quite spectacular. I think you'll love it."

Ida grabbed a shawl and the two of them were off. They walked a short distance to Pioneer Square and hopped on the cable car that ran to Leschi Park. As they rode, Simon shared a bit of history about the park.

"The park was named after Chief Leschi of the Nisqually tribe. They are a Northwest Coastal Indian tribe, whose lifestyle revolves around fishing for salmon and other fish in our coastal waters. They are a proud people who have been treated unfairly in the past."

"I don't understand why people cannot treat others as they would want to be treated themselves. It isn't fair."

Simon refrained from answering as the cable car came to a stop. Ida wasn't ready for it and fell forward into Simon's chest. He put his arms around her, pulling her closer. Tilting her chin up, his head slowly descended until his mouth covered her soft, warm lips.

Oh my.

Kisses from Stefan had never made her heart thump like that, as she felt her breathing hitch. *My word, this man can kiss.* Her body came alive and she became aware of places she'd never thought of before. A throbbing started in her lower body, and she felt a need that she longed to satisfy, if she only knew how. She sighed in his mouth and whimpered as his tongue delved deeper. As soon as she felt she would burst if something didn't happen soon, Simon pulled back, his eyes dark with desire. Ida gazed at him, wide-eyed, and touched her swollen lips.

"I'm sorry. I apologize. I seem to have forgotten where we are."

Ida nodded. She didn't trust herself to speak at the moment.

Flustered, Simon exited the cable car and turned to hold Ida's hand as she stepped down. He held onto her hand as they strolled through the park. Neither of them trusted themselves to speak at the moment. They meandered around the private pathways, enjoying the beautiful flowers and green manicured shrubbery. An immense building, with broad verandas that partially extended out over the water, came into view near the shore of Lake Washington.

"What is that building?" Ida asked.

"That is Leschi Park Pavilion. Many evenings there is dancing in the pavilion, and the residents of Seattle enjoy a bit of music and fun."

"Oh, that sounds lovely. Is there dancing today?"

"I believe there is music planned for this weekend." Simon said. "We could plan on coming back then. We could purchase tickets for a steamboat to take a tour of Lake Washington."

Ida smiled from ear to ear with a smile that lit up her face. "Oh, I have never been on a steamboat. That would be a wonderful experience."

"Are you sure about that? The natives of Seattle believe an enormous and powerful horned snake lives here in these waters," Simon teased.

"Oh, pshaw," Ida said, waving her hand at him. "I don't believe such a thing. I have heard of a monster that lives in Scotland, in Loch Ness. Until I see such a creature with my own eyes, I don't believe such things exist."

"Snakes do not scare you? You are a unique woman."

"Oh, snakes scare me. Especially the ones that walk around on two legs." Ida shuddered. "But your crazy snake myth, *that* doesn't scare me." Ida giggled. "What does a horned snake look like anyway, and is it his horns that make him powerful?"

"Oh, absolutely it's his horns that make him powerful. I bet he is six-feet long and can move faster than you can run. He sneaks up on unsuspecting victims, with his forked tongue flicking in and out and when you least suspect it, he gets you!" Simon jumped at Ida and started tickling her.

"Stop, Simon, stop!" Ida said, giggling and trying to push his hands away. "Stop, I'm so ticklish, oh my goodness, stop." Ida had tears running down her face as she giggled.

Simon chuckled. "I think I have learned a secret weapon against you. It's a good thing I'm not ticklish."

"Oh, aren't you?" Ida swooped in and started tickling him. Simon tried to grab her hands before she could tickle him too much. He pulled her close and gazed at her. Ida shivered from the warmth of his breath.

"You can't get away from me. I won't let you." Simon leaned in and whispered in her ear.

Ida froze, the moment ruined. In her mind, she could hear Stefan knocking on the front door of Elizabeth's house, screaming those same words to her. Her body began to shake and she pulled out of Simon's grasp. "No, no, I won't let you." Ida began to run away from Simon, leaving him startled behind her.

He quickly went after her, reached out to touch her shoulder and turned her toward him. "Ida?" Blank, unfocused eyes stared back at him. "It's me, Simon." He pulled her onto a nearby bench and put his arm around her. "It's all right, honey, everything is going to work out. You're safe. I'm not him. Breathe, sweetheart, breathe. Take a deep breath." He kept repeating those words to her as he rubbed her back, willing her to calm down.

Ida slowly came out of the fog she was in. "I'm sorry. You said those words, and I began to feel a wave of fear. My heart was pounding so loudly, I thought it would come out of my chest. I had to escape and run, I panicked. I've never felt that way before."

"It's called a panic attack." Simon said. "I've heard my mother talk about them from her experience in the battered women's shelter." He paused, as if he didn't want to say more. "And I had several of them, right after Debra died. My vision becomes spotty, and it feels like every wall is closing in on me. I can't catch my breath."

"Yes! That's exactly how it felt."

"Panic attacks are more common than you might imagine. Sometimes there is a reason behind them, such as the loss of a loved one or a violent situation. Sometimes, there's not. The good news, if there is such a thing, is that I'll always be by your side to help you through them. They're an emotional nightmare."

Ida and Simon sat on the bench for a while, holding hands and enjoying the sunshine. Simon knew Ida needed a quiet moment of reflection and safety before moving on. There was a slight breeze off of Lake Washington, and the sun shone brightly in the sky. It was a perfect Seattle day, the kind that he wished would last forever, without a raindrop in sight.

"That mountain is beautiful. Does it have a name?" Ida spoke so quietly, he almost didn't hear her.

"It's Mount Rainier, but it actually isn't a mountain, it's a volcano."

"What? Oh my, is it safe?" Ida looked up at him with huge eyes.

"It last erupted in 1894 and produced small summit explosions, but the past thirteen years have been quiet. It's something we live with, but we don't worry too much about. It's a part of life here."

"Sort of like the powerful horned snake?" Ida said, smiling up at Simon.

Simon laughed out loud. "Exactly! Now, are you ready to join me for dinner?" He stood and held out his arm.

"Absolutely, where are we going?"

"Do you like seafood?"

"I do, although I'm not fond of shellfish."

"There's a little place in the Pike Place Market that I'd like to take you. They have the best seafood around, and I think you'll enjoy it."

They walked back to the cable car, which would take them back to Pioneer Square. From there, they rented a buggy to take them to Pike Place Market. When they arrived, Ida was surprised to see her sister, Elizabeth, along with Max and Harriett Farmer at a table.

"It's so good to see you. What are you doing here?" Ida asked.

Elizabeth laughed. "Your husband arranged this earlier this morning as a little surprise."

Ida turned and looked at Simon in disbelief. "You arranged this?"

He grinned. "I suspected you might want to see more of your sister before she leaves to return to Beckham. I know your time together is limited."

Tears filled her eyes. "You are the sweetest man ever. Thank you."

After a dinner filled with much laughter, Ida and Simon said their good-byes and began the walk home. It was not quite a mile, but the evening was lovely and a romantic stroll was in order after such a filling meal.

Ida held onto Simon's arm as they walked along the Seattle waterfront. "Thank you for a very wonderful evening. I am going to miss Elizabeth a great deal when she leaves. I'm sure her children and her husband can't wait for her to return though. She's never been away from them this long."

"Have the two of you always been close?" Simon realized he didn't know much about his new wife's family.

"Not particularly. Elizabeth is the second oldest child, and I am the youngest. Elizabeth had moved into Beckham before I was born. She couldn't wait to get out of the house with so many children underfoot."

"How many siblings do you have?"

"There are fourteen of us." Ida laughed at the look on Simon's face. "Folks in Beckham called my siblings the demon horde because they tended to get into trouble. The boys more so than the girls, but we were a bit more rambunctious than most."

"That's unbelievable, fourteen kids? Dare I ask what kind of shenanigans your siblings dreamed up?"

"Well, one time my older siblings painted the cow purple. And my brothers tipped over an outhouse with the teacher in it."

Simon looked horrified. "What things did *you* do?"

"Quite honestly, as the baby of the family, I rarely caused trouble. But I was lumped in with my brothers and sisters. As the youngest, I ran the slowest, so adults always caught me and marched me back to my parents to tell them what the demon horde had done now. I believe you could say that I was guilty by association only."

Simon chuckled. "Debra always wanted a large number of children. I used to tell her that it was her only child status that made her want siblings. As one of six myself, I am more than content with two or three children. I guess it doesn't matter how many children she wanted now, does it?" Simon laughed nervously, as if he knew he had ruined the mood.

"No, it doesn't." Ida said quietly. They walked in silence the rest of the way home, arm-in-arm, unaware of the shadow that followed them.

CHAPTER 7

*T*he next few days passed in a blur. Ida fell into a routine of cooking breakfast for her husband and cleaning after he left for work. Thursday had been an interesting day as Mrs. Picklebottom showed up for her regularly scheduled day. Ida and Mrs. Picklebottom had stripped the beds in all of the rooms upstairs and thoroughly washed and cleaned the rooms from top to bottom.

One thing Ida found strange was that she was not allowed to touch the quilt Debra had made. Mrs. Picklebottom insisted that it needed special handling and she would teach Ida how to wash it when the time was right. Ida rolled her eyes when Mrs. Picklebottom wasn't looking and wondered, not for the first time, how in the world she could compete with a ghost! To top it all off, strange things were happening around the house and nobody knew why.

One morning, the back door had been left ajar. Another day, half a loaf of bread had mysteriously disappeared. Ida knew there had been more bread when she went upstairs that evening. At night, Ida swore she could hear footsteps in the attic, but Simon insisted it was probably mice. He scheduled a man to come by and look into it. Ida jumped at every little noise and creak in the floorboard. Her nerves were shot. It didn't help that Elizabeth would soon be leaving to return to Beckham.

On Friday evening, Simon returned from work at six o'clock. Ida was in the kitchen preparing pot roast for dinner. He walked into the kitchen and caught her around the waist, kissing her softly. Ida looked up at him with wide eyes. Was he angry that dinner wasn't on the table?

"I'm hungry, and you look good enough to eat," Simon teased. Ida noticed the twinkle in his eyes.

"Oh, you." Ida swatted him lightly but she secretly enjoyed his attention. She rushed to pull dinner from the oven and carry it out to the table. Simon helped carry the platter with pot roast, carrots and potatoes and set it on the table. Ida grabbed the bread basket and butter and put them out as well. Then, she quickly poured two big glasses of milk and carried them out. She sat down next to Simon.

Once she'd taken her seat, Simon took her hand, and they bowed their heads while Simon said a prayer. As he dished pot roast on his plate, Ida asked, "How was your day?"

"It was full of paperwork, but it kept me busy," Simon said, taking his first bite. He looked at Ida, his eyes twinkling. "This is delicious. I don't know if I've told you, but you are a wonderful cook. Much better than Debra was."

Ida smiled and chose to ignore the last part of his comment. "Why, thank you. I enjoy working in the kitchen and keeping your belly full after a long day of work."

"I was wondering if you might consider enjoying something else with me?" Simon asked.

"What would that be?" Ida suspected she knew where this conversation was heading, and she wasn't sure she was quite ready for that next step.

"I'd like you to consider sharing my bed."

Ida glanced shyly at him, then blushed as she looked at the floor.

"I know you're not certain if you're ready yet. I understand, believe me, I do. But I'd like to share my bed with you and hold you at night. Even if you're not ready for the next step. I won't push you into anything you're not ready for, but I don't want us to sleep apart any longer. Would you consider it?"

Ida nodded. "I'll give you an answer later tonight. But first I hear a few dishes calling my name."

"Sounds fair. I'll be in the sitting room, working on some paperwork. I hope you'll join me by the fire in a bit."

Ida considered his request as she finished washing the dishes from dinner. He was entitled to a wife that shared his bed. It was kind of him to have granted her the four days that she'd already spent in separate sleeping quarters. And he wasn't going to force himself on her but was willing to wait until she was ready.

Truthfully, though, she was quite curious about the marriage bed. Since Elizabeth had explained things to her, she knew there would be pain initially, but she shared that what occurred was a natural joining blessed by God. In marriage, a man is united with his wife in love. Ida had been raised to believe that love never fails, and she believed that with all her heart. Simon was her husband and rightfully, their love must be allowed to grow and flourish.

Ida wiped off the countertops with a washrag one more time. She couldn't put it off much longer. Simon was waiting for her in the sitting room and waiting for an answer. If she wanted to move forward with a true marriage, there really was only one answer she could give.

Ida walked into the sitting room and sat on the sofa. She looked up at Simon. "Would you come sit next to me?"

Simon got up from his desk, crossing the room to sit next to her.

"I thought about what you asked. I'd like to share your bed and be your wife in every way. I find myself laughing and smiling when you are around, and I know that you would never hurt me."

"Hurt you?" Simon was surprised she would think that. "I would never hurt you. You are my wife, and I am to cherish you all the days of our lives. I know Stefan has left scars much deeper than I can see, but I am not him."

Ida took a deep breath. "And I am not Debra. I know you loved her, and I hope there is room in your heart for another."

"What do you mean?"

Ida wasn't sure this was where she meant for the conversation to go, but there was no stopping it now. It needed to be addressed. "This past week you have mentioned Debra quite a bit." Simon started to protest, but Ida was adamant. "Please let me finish."

"I would like to be your wife in every way. I find it difficult to compete with the ghost of another. She is part of your past. I'd like to be your future — the two of us, together, as husband and wife. There's no room in the bed for a third person."

Simon was silent as he stared at the flames in the fireplace.

"Please talk to me, Simon. We cannot move forward in this marriage unless we learn to communicate."

Simon ran his hand through his hair. "What do you want me to say? I have come to care for you a great deal. Yet there are the events of my past that take up space in my mind. I can't forget those memories. I've tried, but turning off my mind is difficult."

Ida grabbed his hand and held it. "I'm not asking you to

forget her. I'm asking you to stop comparing me to her. I'm asking you to stop mentioning her to me in conversation. I want to hear that you care for me and why, but not because I'm similar or different to someone else. Can you do that?"

"I will try. I apologize if I have hurt your feelings. Debra was an important part of my life. By comparing you to her, I thought you would take that as a compliment. I guess I was wrong and I am sorry."

"Oh, Simon," Ida reached over and embraced him. "I'm sorry I didn't speak up sooner. I didn't want to hurt your feelings by bringing it up to you and reopening those wounds." Tears streamed down her face.

Simon kissed her on top of her head and held her in his embrace. The only sound was the crackling of the logs on the fire. Ida settled her head on his chest. It felt so right to be held by him as he stroked her hair.

After a short while, Simon reached out with his hand and tilted her face up to his. He wiped the tears away with his thumb and studied her face. "May I kiss you?"

"I wish you would."

He leaned forward and gently kissed her lips. As she leaned in closer, his tongue traced her lip, and she sighed happily, parting her lips to kiss him back. She felt tingles in the lower half of her belly. Her hands stroked the strong muscles of his back through his shirt.

Simon pulled back, breathing unevenly. Ida stared at him, her beautiful blue eyes large and round. Her hair fell in luscious waves around her shoulders and she looked like an angel. At that moment, he wanted her more than any woman he had ever met.

Simon stood and held out his hand to her. "Would you go upstairs with me?"

Ida took his hand and allowed him to lead her up the stairs to his bedroom. She felt as if she was in a dream she didn't want to wake up from. He closed the door behind them and removed Debra's top quilt from his bed. Ida stood there shyly, not commenting on the action. After placing the quilt on a chair, Simon turned and walked over to her. "You are so beautiful." He leaned down and kissed her softly. "Are you sure you're ready for this? Do you want to wait? I don't want to force you to do anything you're not ready for."

She shook her head. "I'm ready to truly become your wife. I know that you will be patient and gentle with me."

He led her to the edge of the bed and pulled back the blanket. He gently kissed her lips as he pushed her shoulders down so she was sitting on the bed. He laid her back and quickly removed his shirt. He climbed onto the bed with her and kissed her with everything he had in him.

As his tongue moved in her mouth, his hands slowly worked on removing her dress. When she was bare beneath him, he swiftly removed his trousers to lay bare next to her.

Ida felt as if her body was on fire. Every nerve tingled in anticipation of Simon's next move. She trembled under his touch and wished he would end this storm rising up inside her. At the same time, she never wanted this feeling to end — it was amazing. She only knew a little about how the bedroom was supposed to work, but she definitely liked everything she was feeling.

The pleasure was over much too quick. There had been brief pain, but the wave of emotions being intimate had elicited in her were definitely of her liking. If she had ever wondered what floating on a cloud felt like, she knew now.

Ida rolled into Simon, snuggling into his arms. "That was incredible."

Simon lay on his back, holding her tightly. He was still trying to catch his breath from the explosion he had experienced. "You're not allowed to move back into the guest room, you know. I don't think I could survive not having you in my arms from this evening forward. You are so amazingly beautiful. Thank you for coming into my life."

Ida closed her eyes, already drifting asleep. Those weren't the words she wanted to hear, but they were charming nonetheless. As she nodded off to sleep, she knew she had already lost her heart to this wonderful man. She loved him with a fierceness she had never felt before and would never leave him.

CHAPTER 8

*S*aturday morning rolled around. Simon had scheduled a man to come inspect the attic. Since Mrs. Picklebottom was there to help clean, Ida had arranged lunch with Elizabeth and Harriett. Unfortunately, Elizabeth was returning home to Beckham the next day and this was her last visit with her sister. They would pick her up at noon and spend some time shopping afterward.

Ida couldn't wait to get out of the house. She wondered if they had any news on Stefan. He had to be lurking somewhere around Seattle, and that made her nervous. Her breakfast dishes done, she settled in the parlor until the ladies arrived.

A knock on the door startled her. Simon answered it and greeted the inspector. "We're going to head upstairs to the attic. Do you need anything before I disappear?"

"No. Your mother has reserved a twelve-thirty spot at the Seattle Tea Room. We'll do a touch of shopping afterward and be home by dinnertime. Mrs. Picklebottom has instructed me to stay out of the kitchen for the remainder of the day while she fixes something special for us tonight."

Simon walked over and gave her a quick kiss on the lips. "Have fun today, dear. We'll figure out those attic noises and get it fixed for you. And now I'll have that dinner to look forward to tonight." He wiggled his eyebrows and gave her a saucy look as he headed upstairs with the inspector. Ida's laughter followed him.

At exactly twelve o'clock, Elizabeth and Harriett knocked on the door. Ida was ready, and the three of them headed to the nearest cable car. Harriett was a perfect tour guide, sharing the historical changes that had occurred since 1885 when she arrived in Seattle as a mail-order bride herself.

"The Seattle Tea Room is famous for their selection of teas and sandwiches." Harriett shared. "It was opened in 1892 by two sisters. One sister was a wealthy widow and insisted she didn't need to marry again. Instead, she invested her money in the tea room. With the population boom this past ten years, its popularity has increased tremendously."

Elizabeth sighed. "I've fallen in love with this town. I'm going to miss the both of you when I leave tomorrow."

Ida hugged her sister. "We are going to miss you more! Tell me what you've been doing with your time this past week since the wedding. I feel as if we haven't had nearly enough time to be saying our good-byes so soon."

Harriett interrupted. "Oh, this is our stop! Get ready."

The cable car came to a stop, and the three of them stepped off. "Such a convenient way to travel," Elizabeth said. "I think I prefer it over the electric streetcar."

They continued a block down the street and entered the Seattle Tea Room. Inside, they were greeted by two talkative older women, with dark hair and beautiful smiles that lit up the room. Both were about Harriett's age.

"I would like to introduce Elizabeth Tandy, my friend and colleague from Beckham, Massachusetts, who I have told you much about and her sister, Ida Mae Farmer. Ida recently married my son, Simon, and is my new daughter-in-law.

"Ladies, this is Donna Pearson and her sister, Nancy. Donna's husband passed away over seventeen years ago, and she opened this lovely tea room in his memory. She couldn't bear the thought of being with anyone else and needed to support herself."

"It is a pleasure to meet you," Elizabeth said. "I admire female business owners a great deal, being one myself."

Ida shook both of their hands and accepted their congratulations on her new marriage.

"I am so excited to meet you," Nancy Pearson chatted, as she showed them to their table. "Simon is a caring boy who has helped me out with several legal issues in the past. We go to him with all of our troubles. You have chosen well and he is so handsome. It's a shame what he has gone through. Oh, I hope he has shared with you. Well, if not, I won't speak of it further."

Ida smiled and nodded as the woman prattled on. They were seated at a round table near the back of the restaurant. The table provided them with a lovely view of Lake Washington and was fairly private. Nancy continued to ramble on, switching to the weather, until Harriett gently interrupted her.

"Thank you, Nancy, for your hospitality. Do you think we might have a moment to peruse the menu? There are so many lovely choices and I'm sure these two ladies will need a moment to decide." Harriett winked at Ida as Nancy turned.

"Oh, absolutely, dear. You know the menu better than anyone. I won't keep you. It was so nice to meet both of you." Nancy turned away and went to greet the next customers that had come in.

"Whew," Harriett said. "She's sweet and I do love her so. But sometimes you have to stop her from talking all day."

Elizabeth and Ida laughed. Elizabeth teased, "I'm not sure she's the only one who likes to talk."

Harriett chuckled. "I suppose you're right. Now, I want to hear how my new daughter-in-law is doing."

Ida gave her mother-in-law a bright smile. "I am doing well. Simon and I have had minor differences this week, but we've managed to communicate and work through them." She wasn't going to share more than that with Harriett. It wouldn't be proper. "I am concerned though that there may be ghosts in the attic."

Elizabeth and Harriett looked startled. "Whatever do you mean?" Elizabeth asked.

"I keep hearing noises that sound like footsteps. Other mysterious events have been happening. A loaf of bread disappeared, the back door was left open one day, and other food has gone missing as well."

Harriett laughed. "It's probably a pesky raccoon. We had one of those trapped before in our attic. How he got in, I'll never know, but he made quite a mess of the attic space before we caught and relocated him."

"Really?" Ida breathed a sigh of relief. "I was worried there might be spirits in the house."

"It could also be mice," Elizabeth said. "We've had mice before in our home, and Bernard had a difficult time getting rid of them."

"Simon has an investigator there right now going over the attic with him. Raccoon or mice, hopefully they'll be removed by the time I get home. I don't wish to share my home with creatures of nature." Ida shuddered.

Donna Pearson wandered over to take their orders and they settled on a variety of finger sandwiches with the cheese, cracker and fruit tray. All three settled on the green tea, recommended by Harriett.

"So, tell me what you two have been doing with your time

this past week?" Ida asked Elizabeth and Harriett. "I hope you have had a chance to reconnect and swap memories."

Harriett laughed. "We have been sharing our mail order moments. There are many brides and stories that we've shared. Some have made me laugh, and others have left me crying tears of joy."

"Yes," Elizabeth said. "Did I ever tell you about Baby Big Nose?"

"Excuse me?" Ida said, in surprise. "Someone had a baby with a big nose? How awful!"

Elizabeth chuckled. "No, a bride named Merry Winters lost her sister and brother-in-law in a fire. Their two children survived, and Merry took them to raise as her own. She married a man in Mistletoe, Montana, who wanted to find the perfect doll for his new daughter. Her original doll was lost in the fire. Unfortunately, each doll he bought had a flaw and wasn't the right doll. The little girl named them Baby Ugly Hair, Baby Big Nose until he finally found the perfect doll and she named it, Carole."

Harriett was laughing so hard, tears fell from her face. Ida grinned. "I think I like that little girl. What a unique child."

"Speaking of children," Elizabeth said, "Harriett, Max and I spent another day at the Exposition. Did you know you could buy a raffle ticket to win a baby?"

Ida's mouth dropped open. "You mean a doll, right? You can't mean a living, breathing baby?"

Harriett jumped in. "It's true, she means a real baby. That day there was a raffle for a number of prizes, including a month-old orphaned boy named Ernest. He was the property of the Washington Children's Home Society."

"Did you stay for the raffle to see who won?" Ida asked.

"No," Harriett said. "Max wanted to get home, and we couldn't stay. I hope whomever won the poor lad will raise him as their own and treat him right. Too many children are left to fend for themselves these days."

After eating and hearing about the other mail order moments Harriett and Elizabeth had handled over the past twenty-six years, Ida excused herself to use the water closet, near the front of the tea room. After using the facilities, Ida exited the room. Neither of the two sisters were up front at the moment. A man stood with his back to her, looking into the tea room. He was blocking her way back to the table.

"Excuse me, sir." Ida said, trying to be polite but wanting to maneuver around him. "I believe the proprietor will be back shortly to assist you."

The man turned and forcefully grabbed Ida by her arm, pulling her into a side room.

"Fancy meeting you here, you little harlot."

Ida felt the blood drain from her face. "What do you want, Stefan?" she whispered.

He pressed his lips next to her ear and hissed. "You are my bride. You thought you could escape me, but you cannot. I've been watching you and following you. He can't have you, you are mine. Forever."

"It's too late. He is my husband, and I am married now. I want nothing to do with you. I left you because you are pure evil."

Stefan slapped her across the face and squeezed her arm tighter until she cried out in pain. "He will be taken care of. You are mine, and you are coming with me. You've left me quite a mess to clean up, as you've been trolloping around."

"I'm not coming with you," Ida said quietly.

"You are going to go back in there and tell those old hags that you don't feel well and you're going home. Then you are to come back to leave with me."

"And if I don't?" Ida said, defiantly. She was trying to be

brave but her face stung, and she felt a bruise forming already.

"Then I will leave here and find your precious little Simon. It would be a shame to make you a widow so soon. I've been spying on you from that sweltering hot attic all week, waiting for the right time to steal you back. Do not push me, Ida Mae, for your life is worth very little right now."

Ida felt her body shaking. She couldn't let any harm come to Simon. She hadn't even told him yet that she loved him. Their story had just begun, and the ending would not be written by Stefan.

"Stop stalling, woman, and get back to that table. Remember, not one word or your new husband will have a nasty fatal accident." He pushed her out of the side room into the foyer. "Now, go."

Ida stumbled into the dining room, forcing herself to take the steps to return to the table. Her face was pale and drawn and she was sweating profusely.

"Ida? What's wrong? You look awful," Elizabeth stood up from the table and placed her hands on her shoulders.

"I don't feel well. I'm going to head home."

Harriett jumped up. "Oh, we'll go with you."

"No!" Ida shouted. Harriett and Elizabeth looked startled. "I mean, no thank you. It's a short walk to the end of the block, and the cable car runs right by the house. I can make it on my own. I don't want to ruin the rest of your day. You have shopping to do."

Harriett gave her a questioning look. "I know it's a busy city but it's still not a safe place for a lady to walk alone. If you're going, I must insist that we accompany you."

Elizabeth chimed in. "We don't want to see any harm come to you. I couldn't live with myself if something happened."

"I'll be fine," Ida pleaded with them. "Please, you don't have to come."

Harriett and Elizabeth stood. Harriett placed some money on the table to cover the bill and took a hold of Ida's arm. "We insist. Your health and safety is our main concern. Shopping can happen at any time."

As they left the tea room, Ida glanced behind her and saw Stefan following. He glared at her. Ida kept quiet, hoping he would understand that she had no choice in the matter.

As they returned home, Mrs. Picklebottom met them at the door. "Oh dear, what's wrong, Ida?"

"I'm not feeling well. Is Simon around?"

"No, he left in a hurry with the inspector. He didn't say where he was headed. He just rushed right out of here."

Ida turned to Harriett and Elizabeth. "Would you mind if I went upstairs to lie down? Perhaps a rest will help?"

Elizabeth pushed a strand of hair away from Ida's face. "Of course. We can come back later to see how you are doing."

Harriett hugged her. "Rest will do you good. I'm sure when Simon returns, he will take good care of you."

Ida slowly climbed the stairs to their bedroom and sat on the bed. She wasn't sure where Stefan had gotten to but she sensed he was close. How was she going to get out of this mess and where was Simon?

CHAPTER 9

$\mathcal{L}$ ess than ten minutes went by, and the door to the bedroom opened. Stefan stood in the doorway, scowling at her. "Do you think this is a game I'm playing?"

"I'm sorry, they insisted on accompanying me home. I tried to tell them no, but they wouldn't allow it."

Stefan shut the door and walked over to the bed. He grabbed her by the hair and twisted it as he pulled her off the bed onto her knees. He lowered his face in front of her. "You are mine. Even in death, you will be mine. Stand up, you are coming with me." The spittle from his words sprayed her as he talked. "And don't even think of making any noise. You made enough noise in this bedroom last night."

Ida's face burned red, and her anger soared. Who did he think he was, spying on the most intimate act between her and her new husband?

Stefan pulled her over to the window and looked out. He turned back and threw her on the bed. He grabbed the quilt from the foot of the bed, pulled out a knife and began cutting it into strips. As Ida looked on in horror at the destruction of

Debra's quilt, he growled, "Get over here and start tying." He pointed the knife at her. "You don't want to find out what happens if you don't. Then, I'll go out the window, and you will follow me."

~

SIMON WAS FRANTIC. When he and Mr. Daniels inspected the attic, they found signs that someone had been living there. Food remnants and blankets were left behind in the attic, as well as other traces of someone's existence. Simon was horrified. He suspected that it was Stefan. He had to get to Ida and quickly. He wouldn't rest until she was safe and back in his arms. Why had he ignored her complaints and not checked out the attic immediately? *Dear God, please keep her safe.*

He ran down the street and hopped on a cable car. The Seattle Tea Room. That's where she said they were going. He ran his hand through his hair in worry. Why wouldn't this thing go faster?

Finally, it stopped. Simon jumped off and ran down the block to the tea room. He ran inside and saw Miss Nancy and Miss Donna. "Ladies, have you seen my mother?"

"Oh, Mr. Simon, congratulations on your wedding! Your new bride is delightful."

"Yes, thank you." Simon tried not to be rude but he was in a hurry. "Is she here? Have they left yet?"

"Oh dear. Your bride wasn't feeling well and Harriett insisted on accompanying her home. They left a short while ago. You just missed them."

"Thank you, ladies. If you'll excuse me, I'll head home to catch up with them."

Simon left the tea room and ran back to the cable car. As he rode, he felt a strange movement to the cable car. The car came to an abrupt stop, but the movement continued and rapidly became more violent. Simon stared in horror as pieces of buildings began to fall. "No, no, no," he mumbled. "It can't be."

He began to run toward his home, which was difficult as the ground continued shaking. He watched for falling debris as he ran. When he could see his front door, the shaking abruptly stopped. Everything became still again. The damage appeared minimal, but he had to find Ida. He couldn't lose her. He loved her.

He opened the front door of his house and ran inside. "Ida?" he screamed in a panic. "Where are you?"

Mrs. Picklebottom crawled out from underneath the dining table. Simon ran over to help her up. She brushed dust out of her white hair. "Oh, dear. Oh, dear."

"Are you injured, Mrs. Picklebottom?" Simon asked the elderly woman, helping her to a chair. She appeared to be unharmed.

"No, I don't think so. Just shook up." Mrs. Picklebottom laughed hysterically. "Shook up, that's a good one."

"Simon?" He heard his mother's voice coming from the parlor. He left Mrs. Picklebottom sitting at the table and rushed in. Harriett crawled out from underneath the piano, while Elizabeth sat on the sofa fanning her face.

"Where is she? Where is Ida?" Simon looked around the room frantically. "I must find her. I can't lose her."

"She upstairs resting. She wasn't feeling well so we came home. She was very pale."

Shaking, Elizabeth chimed in, "Something is wrong with her. I can't put my finger on it, but she was nervous and acting suspicious on the way home. She kept looking behind us, thinking we wouldn't notice."

Simon turned and ran from the room, taking the stairs two at a time. "Ida?" He shouted, as he got to the top of the stairs. Hearing a whimper, he ran to the bedroom and threw open the door. He was unprepared for the scene before him.

Ida sat in the corner of the room with her knees pulled up. Her head rested on her knees, and she was crying hysterically. The dresser was tipped over, and the room was in disarray from the violent shaking. The worst of it though was the body of a man, hanging out the window. The glass pane of the window had shattered in the earthquake and the pane had fallen on the man. It appeared he had been trying to go out the window, using strips of material tied together, just as the earthquake struck.

"Sweetheart?" Simon said softly, walking over to Ida and sitting down next to her. He pulled her into an embrace, and she sobbed into his shoulder. He held her and rubbed her back as she cried. "I am so grateful you are safe. I'll take a guess that the man is Stefan?"

Ida nodded into his shoulder. As tears flowed down his cheek, Simon closed his eyes. "I thought I'd lost you and would never see you again."

Muffled against him, Ida said, "I'm sorry. I didn't know what to do. He swore he would kill you if I didn't go with him. He's been living in the attic. And worst of all, he destroyed Debra's quilt."

"I don't care about the quilt. I care about you." Simon pulled back. "Look at me."

Ida looked up at him through tear-filled eyes.

"I love you, Ida Mae Farmer. You have wiggled your way into my heart and I can't live without you. I don't want a future without you in it. Will you be my wife?"

Ida giggled. "I already am, silly. I love you, Simon."

Simon pulled her to him and kissed her quickly. "Let's go downstairs before the aftershocks hit. I know Elizabeth and Harriett are worried sick about you."

"What about...him?" Ida gestured to the window.

"Well, he's not going anywhere." Simon said. "I'll contact the police and they can handle the situation. I believe we'll stay elsewhere for a few days."

As Simon and Ida descended the stairs, Max Farmer burst through the front door, looking for Harriett. Upon seeing her, he wrapped her in a giant bear hug and kissed her forehead. "I was so worried."

Harriett rested her head on his chest. "Are the children safe? Did the house survive?"

"Everything is fine. Several pictures fell from the walls and a few dishes were lost, but the children are safe. They are worried about you though."

Harriett and Max kissed. Elizabeth ran up to Ida and pulled her into a hug. "Sit down and tell us what happened."

Ida and Simon relayed the story of Stefan living in the attic and his untimely demise upstairs. Mrs. Picklebottom prepared tea for all their nerves and it was agreed that Simon and Ida would move in with Harriett until the house was again habitable.

EPILOGUE

$\mathcal{I}$da gave her sister a tight hug. "I'm going to miss you so much, Elizabeth." She stepped back with tears in her eyes. "I am so grateful that you convinced me to come to Seattle."

"You and Simon are a match made in, well, in Beckham." Elizabeth laughed. "Regardless of what's in your past, true love always wins. In matters of the heart, nothing is stronger."

Simon hugged his sister-in-law. "Thank you, Elizabeth. You knew exactly what I needed, even though I didn't. I'll take good care of her."

"Of course you will." Elizabeth smiled. "Perhaps one day in the future, Bernard and I will travel back to Seattle to visit with you as your little ones are born."

"Oh, grandbabies! I love that idea." Harriett chimed in. "When do you think you can get me one of those?"

"Mother!" Simon looked embarrassed. "Annabelle will be giving you one of those any day. Don't be greedy!"

Max Farmer took his wife's hand and grinned. "Things happen when we least expect it. Best get prepared, son."

Elizabeth gave each of them one last hug. "Take care of them, Harriett. I'm leaving her in good hands."

Harriett and Ida wiped away tears. Even though Elizabeth would be back for a visit one day, it didn't ease the pain of good-bye.

Elizabeth climbed aboard the train and got settled in her seat, waving at them through the window. The train pulled out of the station on its way back east.

As Max drove the carriage to take them back home, Ida looked around at the beauty of Seattle. Mount Rainier was in the distance, its white cap and rocky walls reminding her that life there would be anything but boring. Ida took Simon's hand in hers, and she couldn't help but wonder what adventure awaited them next. Whatever it was, they would tackle it together.

THE END

~

If you've enjoyed this novel, please consider leaving a review on Amazon. Reader feedback is much appreciated!

Are you looking forward to more books by Cissie Patterson? Here's a sneak peek at *Grace's Hope (Journey to Freedom series)*.

EXCERPT FROM GRACE'S HOPE

PROLOGUE

*G*race Tupper woke up with a start. Something was wrong. In a panic, she threw back the covers and ran into Anna's room. Gone, she was gone, missing! Where could she be? She looked under the bed and in every hiding spot she could imagine. "Anna? Where are you, baby?"

She looked outside. The fog was rolling in across the field and covered the land in a fine mist. Grace quickly grabbed her shawl and ran outside. She pulled the shawl tightly around her shoulders. She had to be here, she had to be close. Grace knew she couldn't give up looking. Her baby was out there - there was nowhere else she could be.

"Mama?" Anna's tiny voice, quivering in fear, sounded from nearby. Grace could picture Anna's tiny bottom lip shaking as tears flowed down her face. Anna was only three and she needed her mother.

"I'm here, baby. Mama's right here. Where are you?"

Grace looked around but the fog was closing in too thick to see. Where could she be, she sounded so close. "Anna?"

"Mama?" Anna's voice sounded further away instead of closer. Where was she? "Papa, I can't find Mama." Grace heard her husband's voice whispering harshly to Anna and the sound of a slap as her daughter began to cry. Something was wrong. Something was very wrong.

"Henry?" Grace demanded. Silence, nothing but silence. Where were they? She had to find them. "Henry!" Grace cried out again. The fog surrounded her, engulfing her like the smothering smoke of wet logs on a fire. As leaves rustled to her right, Grace turned her head and listened. Where were they?

"You'll never find her." Henry's voice sounded close, like she could almost reach out and touch him. "She's gone from you. I told you never to cross me, but you wouldn't listen. You couldn't do what I told you to do, you never do. This is all your fault, rotten witch. You will never see your daughter again." A rush of air flew by Grace's head and she turned. Out of the fog, she saw a dark shadow coming, but she couldn't dodge it. The heavy blow hit her in the head, and Grace fell. Her last memory was of Henry standing over her snarling, "You will *never* see your precious Anna again."

CHAPTER ONE

*G*race awoke with a start. The sound of the train wheels reminded her of all she'd lost – *you can't go back, you can't go back, you can't go back*. Grace's eyes filled with tears as she stared out the window at the rain. This awful rain – she'd been on this train for three days now, and the rain had started to fall within the first few hours of her journey. It matched her gloomy mood and most likely brought on the nightmare again — the day life as she knew it ended.

Two years had gone by. Two years since she had last seen her darling Anna. If she only would have known when she put her to bed that night, that Henry would reappear and take their daughter away. She didn't know where her baby was. She didn't know if Anna was alive or dead — she only knew that she had to find a way to keep on living.

She couldn't keep living in that town, in the place where her dreams were stolen from her. Oh, she'd tried, hoping that Anna would somehow find her way back to her. Every day she'd watch out the window or sit outside under the tree, waiting and watching with tears streaming down her cheeks. And then one day, they had come.

Sheriff Hutson rode aside a wagon, pulled by two men whose names she couldn't remember. A wagon, with something in the back. She recalled the slow speed of it and the heat of the day. A fly flew around her face, landing ever so often and crawling across her arm. The smell of dry, burnt grass turned her stomach, as the wagon drew closer and closer.

When it pulled up next to her, she remembered Sheriff Hutson asking her to identify the body within. The body of Henry, her good-for-nothing, vile husband. The man who told her she'd never be good enough, never be enough wife or mother, never be enough of anything to keep his malicious side happy. But Anna, where was Anna?

Grace remembered shrieking like a mad-woman. She remembered Sheriff Hutson holding her back as she beat at him, screaming for her daughter, beseeching him to find her baby. She remembered the doctor coming out to give her some sort of medicine, and her neighbor, Penny, wiping her brow. She existed, going through the motions, until one day she woke up and knew she had to leave. Her life here was over.

As the train ride entered into its third evening, Grace pulled out the letter and read it again. The letter that gave her courage to begin a new life, a life out West, a life where happiness would still elude her but a fresh start was guaranteed. A life with Charlie Thornton in Freedom, Colorado.

Future bride,

Are you looking for a new life? A life filled with choices and freedom to be yourself? I am looking for someone to join me in Colorado. I own my own claim, and it is doing well. I am looking for a female who wishes to experience the western adventure.

If you are between the ages of twenty and twenty-five, are able to cook and manage a home, then I am looking for you. A desire to have children is a bonus but not a requirement.

I am willing to support you as we discover each other's interests. Let's not fool ourselves into believing love will be immediate. We must grow together as friends first as we develop a mutual respect. If this arrangement interests you, please reply to me in Freedom, Colorado.

Charlie Thornton

Freedom. Freedom! If ever God was talking to her, this letter was it. Grace needed to escape and find freedom. She had saved a little money of her own and if Charlie Thornton wasn't the man for her, she'd forge a new life for herself. She was free of Henry and his controlling ways. She was free to begin again and maybe, just maybe, she'd find a way to be free to forgive herself for losing Anna.

AFTERWORD

Dear Reader,

Thank you so much for purchasing and reading *Mail Order Moments*. I hope you enjoyed the story of Simon Farmer and Ida Mae Miller. This book has been a dream of mine since I read the Brides of Beckham series by Kirsten Osbourne. I've constantly wondered what happened to the brides, would Harriett and Elizabeth keep in touch, what happened in their lives. Without Kirsten Osbourne's support and gentle nudging, this book would never have been written. Along the way, other authors encouraged my writing endeavors and I am eternally grateful.

Much research has gone into the history of Seattle at this time period. In the summer of 1909, a world's fair, the Alaska-Yukon-Pacific Exposition, took place on the grounds of the University of Washington. Opening Day, June 1, was declared a city holiday, and 80,000 people attended. By the time the fair closed on October 16, over 3,700,000 had visited. Controversy surrounded many of the exhibits of the World's Fair and all exhibits are factual as described. A month-old orphaned boy named Ernest was raffled away as a prize. Although a winning ticket was drawn, nobody claimed the prize. The ultimate destiny of the child was still being investigated in 2009.

For the purpose of **Mail Order Moments**, I took some literary license with the timing of the Seattle earthquake. A 6.0 earthquake did occur in Seattle in 1909, however, factually this earthquake occurred in January. For the purpose of the book, this author did adjust the timing of the event.

The 1906 San Francisco earthquake struck the coast of Northern California at 5:12 a.m. on April 18. Devastating fires soon broke out, including the *Ham and Eggs* fire, and burned for several days. It has been estimated that up to 90% of the total destruction was the result of the subsequent fires. When it was all over, approximately 3,000 people died and over 80% of San Francisco was destroyed. The events are remembered as one of the worst and deadliest natural disasters in the history of the United States. Reconstruction was largely completed by 1915, in time for the 1915 Panama-Pacific International Exposition, which celebrated the reconstruction of the city and its "rise from the ashes".

If you like this story, please consider leaving a review. Reviews are never expected but always appreciated. I look forward to sharing more stories with you as I continue writing **Grace's Hope**, book one of my new *Journey to Freedom* historical romance series.

Made in the USA
San Bernardino, CA
14 April 2018